TEACHING KIDS TO CARE AND TO BE CAREFUL

A Practical Guide for Teachers, Counselors, and Parents

John C. Worzbyt

ScarecrowEducation
Lanham, Maryland • Toronto • Oxford
2004

Published in the United States of America
by ScarecrowEducation
An imprint of The Rowman & Littlefield Publishing Group, Inc.
4501 Forbes Boulevard, Suite 200, Lanham, Maryland 20706
www.scarecroweducation.com

PO Box 317
Oxford
OX2 9RU, UK

British Library Cataloguing in Publication Information Available

Library of Congress Cataloging-in-Publication Data

Worzbyt, John C.
  Teaching kids to care and to be careful : a practical guide for teachers,
counselors, and parents / John C. Worzbyt.
      p. cm.
  Includes bibliographical references and index.
  ISBN 1-57886-137-3 (pbk. : alk. paper)
  1. Moral education. 2. Caring—Study and teaching—Activity programs.
  3. Children—Conduct of life. I. Title.
  LC268.W76 2004
  370.11'4—dc22
  2004000898

CONTENTS

PREFACE

Teaching Kids to Care and to Be Careful is designed to help children care more deeply, manage risk more responsibly, and experience life more fully. Helping children to meet these basic needs is of vital interest to all people who want children to enjoy life to the fullest in a climate of caring and safety. We want our children to be around tomorrow and to grow into responsible, caring, and contributing members of society.

Some people have described caring as the ultimate driving force that makes us human and gives life purpose and meaning. To care is to show concern and interest in oneself, others, and the environment. It is central to all life decisions; it is the unifying force that brings relevancy and purpose to learning.

Children must be taught the value of caring and how to give and receive care. They must likewise learn to recognize danger and how to exercise due care in a world that is not always kind and caring (Worzbyt, O'Rourke, & Dandeneau 2003).

Caring represents "the activities, relationships, examples, and services offered to young people which support their development and the attitudes, values, and behaviors that young people develop that in turn position them to value and participate in social service, social justice, and social change" (Pittman & Cahill 1992, 39). Thus, caring is an energizing, life-shaping force in which children first experience being cared for and then learn how to care for themselves and others.

The lessons presented in *Teaching Kids to Care and to Be Careful* are the following:

- Treat others as you yourself would like to be treated.
- Those who learn to care make caring choices.
- Caring gives life purpose and meaning—it is the glue that binds people together in caring communities.
- Caring can be a gratifying act of choice, a burden, a commitment to action, dangerous, and a life-changing experience for givers and receivers alike.

CHAPTER-BY-CHAPTER DESCRIPTION OF THIS BOOK

These life lessons come alive in six practical, energy-packed, and caring chapters full of useful ideas, easy-to-use activities, and caregiving tips:

- My Life Has Value
- Seven Centers of Care
- Helpful Habits—Hurtful Habits
- Caring and Danger
- Learning to Be Careful
- Giving and Receiving Care

Chapter 1: My Life Has Value teaches children the value of life and helps them to recognize value in themselves. They learn that people care for what they value and thus discover a multitude of reasons to care for themselves and others.

Chapter 2: Seven Centers of Care teaches children that they live in a world community of caregivers and receivers of care. They learn that the balance of nature is dependent on the caring choices they make in the seven centers of care. They likewise learn that they have much to give and to receive as valued and contributing family, classroom, school, and community members.

Chapter 3: Helpful Habits—Hurtful Habits encourages children to identify and explore the many habits they have developed in the seven centers of care. They learn the value of habits and that some are helpful and others hurtful, and they learn how to stop practicing hurtful habits and instead learn ones that will be helpful and caring in the seven centers of care.

Chapter 4: Caring and Danger teaches children that caring is not without danger to themselves, others, and the environment. They learn the meaning of danger and how to identify danger in the seven centers of care. Children learn that while danger is always present in the world, it is not to be feared, as they can learn to make caring choices in the context of being careful.

Chapter 5: Learning to Be Careful focuses on risk-taking and risk management. Children learn that risk-taking is a normal part of life, living, and caring. They also discover the importance of learning to become responsible risk managers in lowering danger to themselves, others, and the environment and how to increase caring and safe outcomes by virtue of the choices they make.

Chapter 6: Giving and Receiving Care helps children maximize their potential as caring human beings. It provides them with the opportunity to experience the personal joy and well-being that comes from caring for themselves, and to experience the purpose and meaning in life that comes from helping others to care and be careful.

Teaching Kids to Care and to Be Careful has become a labor of love. It is a mission that unites homes, schools, and communities together in caring and community building. As important as caring is to our children and the planet, it cannot be left to chance. Caring must become the first job of homes, schools, and communities, to "nurture the growth of competent, caring, loving, and loveable persons" (Noddings 1992, vii).

So why wait? Take the first step and experience the excitement and enthusiasm I have enjoyed in exploring the vast untapped opportunities in teaching children to care and be careful. Your children will thank you for helping them find purpose and meaning in their lives. And the world will thank you for children who truly care.

TIPS FOR USING THIS BOOK

Teaching Kids to Care and to Be Careful is designed and organized for easy use. Each chapter begins with a brief *Definition* of a key caring concept to be introduced, followed by *Background Information* that provides helpful insight and understanding regarding the intent of each chapter and the goals to be addressed. Next comes the *Role of Facilitator,* which highlights the significance of each chapter and offers tips and suggestions regarding how to introduce and teach each caring concept. *Activities* are then provided that support and reinforce children's understanding, application, and appreciation of the caring concept in review.

The last two sections of each chapter provide additional reinforcement in teaching the caring concept. *Suggestions for the Week* help teachers integrate the caring concept into their academic curriculum so children will understand and be able to relate how what they are learning in each subject relates to their becoming caring children and builders of caring communities. *Tips for Caregivers* is designed for home use and provides parents and caregivers with a condensed version of each chapter, complete with activities. Families can thus become active participants, working in partnership with the school in teaching children to care.

To help you and your children gain as much from this book as possible, I offer the following tips and suggestions in teaching children to care and to be careful:

- Introduce each chapter in sequence, starting with chapter 1 and ending with chapter 6, as the caring concepts being taught reinforce each other.
- Spend no less than one week introducing each chapter concept. While the concepts can be taught and understood by children in less than an hour using the activities provided, they need time and opportunities to practice what they are learning.
- Use *Suggestions for the Week* to reinforce each caring concept. This can be done without taking additional teaching time away from your already busy teaching schedule. Your goal is to help your children understand that what they are learning in school relates

directly to their becoming caring people and builders of caring communities. When you help them make this connection through your teaching, they will understand how what they are learning relates to life and living in and outside the classroom.

- I encourage you to involve the home in teaching children to care and to be careful. *Tips for Caregivers* can be reproduced and given to family members along with a letter of explanation of how to use these tips. Better yet, encourage your school counselor and parent-teacher organization to offer a six-week evening workshop series on teaching children to care using the *Tips for Caregivers* as the basis for this training.

- Community involvement in teaching children to care is important. This can be accomplished throughout the six chapters. However, chapter 6 will be especially helpful as it provides many suggestions for involving children in home, school, and community caring projects.

- *Teaching Kids to Care and to Be Careful* is a never-ending process. A lifetime of activity can be spent reinforcing the caring concepts taught in this book. You will never run out of material, activities, and projects for teaching your children to care. Once you have taught these six chapters, continue to use this book to stimulate and generate your own innovative ideas in teaching children to care.

- As you teach your children to care, consider developing a home, school, and community partnership complete with a steering committee to provide children with opportunities to give and receive care at home, in school, and in their community.

- Lastly, use this book as a guide and a resource. Feel free to modify activities and substitute your own activities when you choose to do so. Make this book your blueprint for teaching children to care and to find purpose and meaning in their lives as caring human beings.

As a parent, grade school teacher, elementary school guidance counselor, and counselor of education, I have devoted 39 years of my life to helping children live full and productive lives. Only in recent years have I discovered the importance of teaching children to care. Caring is central to all life decisions; it is the unifying force that brings meaning and purpose to life and living, and brings relevancy to teaching and learning.

I therefore believe that a quality education is accomplished when children and educators alike (home, school, and community) recognize that all teaching and learning is about preparing children to make caring choices in the context of being careful so they may care more deeply, manage life's risks more responsibly, and experience life more fully as caring people and builders of caring communities.

ACKNOWLEDGMENTS

Teaching Kids to Care and to Be Careful has been about helping children find meaning and purpose in their lives as givers and receivers of care. It has been about helping them personally experience the joys of life and living through giving. And it has been about helping children become caring human beings and builders of caring communities.

Caring is at the core of our nature; it is what we are destined to do. I have learned much about my caring self and human nature in writing this book, and I have learned that we live in a world where there is far more caring than I ever imagined possible.

As I reflect on my life, past and present, I can now fully appreciate all I have received from those who have cared for me. It is these people I want to recognize, for in many ways they too are the authors of *Teaching Kids to Care and to Be Careful.*

To my parents, I am particularly grateful for your love and guidance in teaching me to give and receive care and to live life to the fullest.

To my wife, Jean, and my two children, Jason and Janeen, thank you for teaching me the value of family and the life lessons learned in what it means to be a loving spouse and a caring parent.

To my colleagues, Drs. Kathleen O'Rourke and Claire Dandeneau, with whom I have written and taught, thank you for your caring nature in helping me challenge my thinking, develop my ideas, and express a sense of caring through my writing.

To Susan Sibert and Francine Endler, in their respective roles as elementary school principal and supervisor of guidance services, thank you for providing me with invaluable feedback and suggestions that have enhanced the value of this book in meeting the needs of teachers, counselors, and parents as they seek to teach children to care and be careful.

To my former graduate assistants, Amy Borick, Jennifer Hadel, Jana Hardee, Barbara Rhine, Nancy Rowse, Heather Sakala, Cally Scott, and Megan Schoenfeld, thank you for your typing assistance, trips to the library, research assistance, and continued support. And to Andrea Epple and Erin-Caitlin Rinker, my principal research assistants, I owe a sincere debt of gratitude for long hours of work and unwavering commitment. Without your assistance, this book would never have become a reality.

To Cindy Tursman, managing editor at ScarecrowEducation, thank you for your kind words and the opportunity you have provided me in helping others to teach children the value of caring. I would also like to thank Marjorie K. Johnson, assistant editor, for her words of encouragement and Kellie Hagan, production editor, for all she has done in helping me to create a quality book in a timely manner. I am especially grateful for Kellie's understanding and guidance. She has been my caregiver throughout this process.

And lastly, I would like to recognize Jane Washburn, former colleague, lifelong friend, and caregiver who encouraged me to write this book. It has taken me 32 years to fulfill her wish and it is to her that I dedicate this work.

To each and every person who reads this book, I hope you are inspired to pass on to the children in your life a legacy of caring and community building. They will appreciate it and the world will be forever indebted to you.

①

MY LIFE HAS VALUE

DEFINITION

Value: That quality of anything that renders it desirable or useful and worthy of care.

BACKGROUND INFORMATION

Most children learn from a very early age that money has value (worth). Consequently, when children receive money, they place value on it and care for it. They place it in a safe and secure location until they are ready to exchange it for something they want.

While most children understand the value of money, many have not learned the same lesson with respect to placing value on themselves and their lives. Children who fail to learn this valuable life lesson are not likely to make caring and responsible life choices on behalf of themselves or others.

As caring adults in children's lives, we want them to recognize that life does have value. We want them to love and care for themselves and to experience self-worth. We want them to live a life of purpose and meaning as caring human beings and builders of caring communities.

Children are, by nature, caring individuals. However, their caring nature must be nurtured by loving and caring adults if their true nature is to be realized. The goal of this chapter is to help you teach children that life does have value, in particular, their lives. Together, we can help children to develop their full potential as givers and receivers of care. If we as a society are to pass on to our children a legacy that values the sanctity of human life, we must help our children to discover value in themselves and teach them how to care.

Helping Children to Discover Their Value

People who love and value themselves demonstrate this in their actions. They make their health and happiness top priorities. They love themselves unconditionally and strive to meet their needs and wants through caring choices that are based on *Right, Reality,* and *Responsibility. Right* choices are legal (based on law), ethical (meet societal standards of conduct), and moral (meet personal standards of basic goodness). *Reality* choices are supported by evidence that dispel the possibility of myth. *Responsible* choices produce consequences that are judged to be desirable and safe for the decision maker and those touched by the decisions.

Children learn about themselves and life itself from their teachers (parents and caregivers). This process begins early in childhood, when children begin to view themselves as being good or bad, accepted or rejected, and useful or devalued family members. They learn that their world is a friendly or hostile place; they develop feelings of confidence, encouragement, and self-assuredness or become fearful, guilt-ridden, discouraged, and disconnected.

Children's sense of self depends so much on the treatment they receive and their perceptions of it. So what can we do to help children value themselves and their lives? What can we do to help them to become caring human beings who embrace the importance of making caring choices for themselves and for others?

Helping children to value themselves begins with understanding how they come to view themselves. Two of the most widely used terms that provide insight into self are *self-concept* and *self-esteem.* Although self-concept and self-esteem are very much related, they are not without differences. Self-concept describes how children *think* about themselves, while self-esteem relates to how children *feel* about themselves. When these two concepts interact, children are able to assess their self-worth (the value they place on themselves).

Children may *think* about themselves globally or, more specifically, in terms of their physical, emotional, social, intellectual, and spiritual self. Consequently, children may describe (self-concept) themselves as being short or tall (physical), shy or outgoing (emotional), having many friends or few friends (social), being smart or academically challenged (intellectual), and living a life of purpose or confusion (spiritual). How children *feel* about themselves in these self-defining areas evolves from their evaluation of self, in which they ask themselves the question, "How am I doing?" If Billy places high value on being a good student but views himself to be academically inadequate, his emotional sense of self will suffer (self-esteem), and he will devalue himself (self-worth) in this area of his life. If by contrast the opposite is true and Billy views himself as a good student, he will view his emotional sense of self as positive.

Children who value themselves and lead their lives in a caring and responsible manner possess a realistic, fact-supported view of themselves and an ideal self (what they strive to be) that is challenging but not out of reach. For example, Tom, a fifth-grader, pictures himself as having athletic ability in football despite some skill deficits that he hopes to address (fact-supported view of self). He images himself as he would like to be—a skilled football player (ideal self)—and strives to improve himself through realistic goal setting and hard work. Tom is likely to experience a positive emotional sense of self (self-esteem), knowing that he is making progress toward a realistic, challenging goal that is based on self-improvement rather than perfection. Positive self-worth is therefore contingent upon children developing accurate and self-caring opinions and realistic perceptions and expectations of themselves in transition.

Teaching Children to Value Themselves and Life

Children who value themselves and their lives are striving to know good, to be good, and to do good. They are effective self-managers who invest in themselves by making responsible caring choices that will enhance their physical, emotional, social, intellectual, and spiritual selves while striving to assist others in appreciating the value of life and living.

When children value themselves and life, they become caring, loving, loveable, and responsible human beings. They know who they are and that they are accepted by others, and more importantly, they are acceptable to themselves. They are developing a self-identity steeped in self-worth, one that is based on a realistic, fact-supported perceived self and an ideal self that is challenging but not out of reach.

Children learn that their lives have value because of who they are—living human beings. Secondly, they learn that their lives have value based on what they can be and do as givers and receivers of care. Helping children to develop their human potential can be best illustrated by focusing on Erikson's (1963) psycho-social stages of human development and the impact that nurturing has on how children come to value themselves, others, and life. The four stages of development that most significantly impact children's lives from birth to age twelve are Basic Trust versus Mistrust (birth to age eighteen months), Autonomy versus Shame and Doubt (ages eighteen months to three years), Initiative versus Guilt (ages three to six), and Industry versus Inferiority (ages six to twelve).

Basic Trust versus Mistrust *birth - 18 months*

Children need to develop trust in their environment and in the people who care for them during their first eighteen months of life. When trust is established, children feel safe and secure in their surroundings. They likewise experience a friendly, predictable, and consistent environment. If this outcome is to be achieved, children need parents and caregivers who provide for their physical and emotional needs, and do so in a caring, consistent, and predictable manner.

When parents and caregivers fail to meet children's needs and do not provide affectionate, high-quality care, these children will experience a sense of mistrust toward their caregivers, others, and the world. Interpersonal relationships are likely to suffer or fail to form in children who do not trust.

Autonomy versus Shame and Doubt *18 months - 3 yrs.*

From eighteen months to three years of age, children strive to gain control over their own being and surroundings. Children in this stage of development strive to experience success in doing things for themselves. They express a sense of autonomy through language, motor development, and behaviors. Children use words like "no," "me," "mine," and "I" to express their independence. They learn to walk, talk, dress, and feed themselves, and they practice toilet behaviors as they strive for autonomy.

To achieve a sense of autonomy, children need parents and caregivers who provide opportunities for them to experience success in doing things for themselves (walking, talking, eating, dressing, and helping around the house). Absent these experiences of guided self-expression and experimentation, children are likely to lose the struggle between feelings of autonomy and self-doubt and shame. When children are not given the opportunity, by overly critical or protective parents, to make mistakes, try again and succeed, test the limits, and explore their potential, they foster dependence, discouragement, fear, and a loss of spontaneity. These factors tend to foster shame and doubt and cause children to disconnect from themselves and others. These children experience difficulty in finding their places in their families and in the world. They are thus hampered in their development of self.

Initiative versus Guilt   3-6 yrs.

From three to six years of age, children strive to develop a sense of initiative and competence (a take-charge lifestyle) versus feelings of guilt that arise when they believe they can't do anything right. Thus children are motivated to fulfill their need to belong and to become respected and caring family members. They are eager to participate in meaningful family activities and projects, learn socially accepted interpersonal skills, set goals, and develop social interests that foster cooperation and inclusion.

If children are to develop initiative, they need parents and caregivers who will give them the freedom and guidance to self-explore and who will nurture their sense of empowerment by involving them in family outings, activities, projects, work, and discussions. They likewise need caring parents and teachers who will provide structure, discipline, and guidance in shaping the lives of their children into responsible and caring ones.

When children are not given the opportunity to develop initiative, they are likely to have a negative view of themselves, fear making decisions, allow others to choose for them, and experience a sense of guilt and powerlessness. They devalue themselves and struggle to find acceptance and a life of purpose in a world that seems devoid of both.

Industry versus Inferiority *6-12 years*

During the next six years of life (ages six to twelve), children have a need to expand their view of the world and the skills they will need to make their place in it. They struggle to develop a basic belief in their own competence and to achieve a sense of self-worth that comes from repeated life successes and accomplishments. Failure to understand the world and to learn basic academic and life skills needed to achieve a sense of industry compromises children's ability to set and attain personal goals. Failure to achieve success results in feelings of incompetence, inferiority, and discouragement.

If children are to develop a sense of industry, they need loving parents and caregivers who teach them the physical, emotional, social, intellectual, and work skills required to succeed in school and in life. These same children also need lots of love, large doses of encouragement, and an abundance of praise in support of their quest to achieve competence, independence, and self-worth in a world that relies on givers and receivers of care.

When children receive the love and support of parents, teachers, and other caregivers, they will develop a sense of trust, autonomy, initiative, and industry. They will have a positive self-image, an understanding of who they are, what they want to be, and what they have to give as caring children and builders of caring communities. They will be goal directed, focused, and self-assured. They will be developing an identity that gives their life purpose, meaning, and direction. They will love themselves, experience the love of others, and love life as givers and receivers of care. They will enter the stage of Identity versus Role Confusion (ages twelve to eighteen) prepared to attain a clear realization of themselves and their potential; they will develop a caring identity and a utilization of self full of promise and good works.

ROLE OF FACILITATOR

Your role is to help children to recognize that life has value and that their lives have value too. Help them to develop an awareness of the multitude of caring choices made every day that demonstrate the value of life. Many of these caring choices have touched and improved the quality of their lives as well. Help children to explore their own potential as caring human beings and to care for what they value.

Your role is exciting, challenging, and full of promise, for you will be helping children to value life and to love themselves. This is what makes life worth living. At first glance, the task of teaching children to love themselves and to value life may seem overwhelming. Where do I begin, you might ask? The journey begins, like all journeys, with the first step.

The good news regarding your task is that self-worth and the value of life are by-products of a successful life. Children place value on themselves and life itself in a life-long process that has its beginning in childhood, where their lives are nurtured, allowing nature to take its true course.

The research of Erikson (1963), Havinghurst (1972), and Maslow (1954) has collectively demonstrated that it is in children's nature to meet their own physical, emotional, social, intellectual, and spiritual needs. It is in their nature to trust and to develop a sense of autonomy, initiative, and industry that gives purpose and meaning to their lives. Also, it is in their nature to love themselves and to value lives, as those of givers and receivers of care. The seeds of self-worth, a love of life, and a caring personality are already in place but need to be brought forth by loving caregivers like yourself.

There are four life-defining questions that I want you to consider in your facilitator role. The answers to these questions will guide you in helping children achieve success at home, in school, and in life. As children develop competence and achieve success as givers and receivers of care, they will experience the by-products of a purposeful and meaningful life, self-worth, and a love of life. These questions are:

1. What do you want to *be*?
2. What do you want to *do*?
3. What do you want to *have*?
4. What do you want to *give*?

What Do You Want to Be?

Children want to *be* a variety of things. They want to *be* accepting of themselves, to be accepted by others, safe, secure, and happy. Most of all, they want to *be* caring human beings and builders of caring communities. This is in their nature. Children thus have a need to *be* connected to themselves, other human beings, and their surroundings. Developing caring connections in these three areas of life helps children achieve a sense of safety, security, belonging, self-esteem, and predictability in their lives. Children learn to place trust in themselves, others, and their surroundings and to invest in their connections through caring choices.

When children's connections are threatened or broken, they are likely to experience fear, isolation, loneliness, and a general loss of security. Broken toys, divorce, death, loss of a friendship, a change in surroundings, illness, and harsh criticism are examples of life experiences that can cause disconnections that decrease personal comfort, increase stress, and negatively impact self-esteem.

Your role as a facilitator is to help children determine what they want to *be*. Help them to see the value in becoming a caring person and a builder of caring communities. Help them to connect with the joy that comes from being a caregiver and a receiver of care. Help them to connect with the caring choices they can make in building caring connections with themselves, others, and their environment.

What Do You Want to Do?

Doing leads to being. If you want children to fulfill their nature as caring human beings and builders of caring communities, they must learn to *do* what caring people do. Children cannot build caring connections with themselves, others, or the environment in the absence of knowing what to *do*. Children who want to *be* friends with others must *do* the things that friends do. They must engage in acts of friendship. Wants and needs are achieved through *doing*; the by-products of *doing* are success, self-worth, and a life of value.

Children need to develop physical, emotional, social, intellectual, and work skills that will enable them to build caring connections with themselves, others, and their surroundings. For example, smiling is a caring social skill that can be used to build friendship connections. When children lack (in quality or quantity) caring skills and attributes or develop traits that are unacceptable to others, they are thwarted in their ability to build meaningful and responsible connections. These children are likely to experience feelings of low personal self-worth, rejection, depression, and loss of interest in life.

Your role as facilitator is to help children understand the power of *doing* in helping them achieve what they want to *be*. Help children to understand that if they want to become caring human beings, to achieve success as givers and receivers of care, they must use their caring skills, assets, and personality characteristics.

What Do You Want to Have?

Children are motivated to achieve their needs and wants because there is a payoff in it for them. For example, children who want to *be* friends with others and *do* the things that friends do will *have* friends. Children who strive to *be* givers and receivers of care and *do* what caring people do will have caring attributes that they can call their own.

What children *have* comes from what they *do*. Sometimes children *have* things they would like to eliminate or remove (a bad reputation, guilt, fear, loneliness, and so on). Billy has low grades and would like to *have* high grades. Billy can *be* a good student by *doing* what good students do, and if he does, his grades will improve along with his self-esteem and his love of life.

As facilitator, you can help children to decide what they want to *have* in life and how to achieve it. You can help them examine what they currently *have* and want to keep (specific life skills, a good reputation, desired personality characteristics); you can help them examine what they *have* that they would like to give up (anger, low self-esteem, guilt, self-doubt) and show them how to do it. You can help them determine the degree to which their *haves* and *have nots* impact the quality of their lives and what they can *do* to enhance their potential as caregivers and receivers of care.

What Do You Want to Give?

Children can only *give* to others what they *have*. The joys of life and living are in the *giving*. Human beings were meant to be *givers* and receivers of care. This is their purpose for being. This is what *gives* life value and meaning.

Children are meant to *be* caring human beings and builders of caring communities. If children's nature is nurtured in this direction, they will learn to *do* what caring people do. With practice, they will *have* caring assets and attributes that are fully developed and that they can *give* to themselves, others, and society. Life takes on value when we "pass on" the best that we *have* to *give*. By *giving* away what they *have*, children take their place in the circle of care and reap the benefits of *having* a life of purpose and meaning.

Unfortunately, children also "pass on" the worst of themselves. These *givers* pay a high price for their actions. They experience discouragement, loss of self-worth, and lives devoid of purpose and meaning.

As a facilitator, help children to understand the value of *giving*. Encourage them to *give* the very best that they *have* to offer. Help them to understand that in defining themselves as caregivers and builders of caring communities, they also contribute to their own well-being and lives of value.

The activities that follow teach that *life does have value*. These experiences are designed for children of all ages, and they address the concepts of *human worth* and the *value of life*. They help children understand that their lives do have value; they emphasize to children the importance of caring for what they value. Help children make classroom-to-life connections by demonstrating that what they are learning in school is the value of caring. *Suggested Activities for the Week* provide some *useful ideas* for addressing this point. Have fun with this chapter and the activities that follow in teaching children the *value of life*. Continue to emphasize this concept—*life has value*—in all that you do.

BENEFITS TO CHILDREN

Children who value themselves and life:

- Care for what they value
- Think before they act
- Live a life of purpose and meaning, caring for themselves and others.

PITFALLS FOR CHILDREN

Children who do not recognize the value of human life:

- Engage in high-risk behaviors
- Act without thinking
- Place their lives and the lives of others in danger.

ACTIVITIES

My Life Has Value

Objectives

1. To help children understand they have value and are valued.
2. To help children to identify what gives their lives value and worth.
3. To help children care for what they value in themselves.

Group Size: Classroom group
Time Required: 15–30 minutes
Materials: $100 bill ($20 bill can be used)
Facilitator: Most children understand what gives money value, but they are less likely to understand how to equate (measure) value in themselves. The purpose of this activity is to help children recognize they have value, identify value in themselves, and explore ways in which they can care for themselves. Help your children to recognize that while most people care for money and other material things, they may not care for themselves. Your goal is to help your children learn to love, value, and care for themselves.

Process

1. Introduce the word *value* to children by using it in a sentence: "A $100 bill ($20) has *value*." Ask them to define the word. Write their ideas on the chalkboard.
2. Present your children with the following situation. Ask them to form a circle (while standing). Place either a $100 or $20 bill in the

center of the circle. Tell your class to pretend that this bill belongs to them. Ask them, "If this was your $100 bill and you noticed it on the floor, would you leave it there or pick it up?"

3. Most children will tell you they would not leave the money on the floor. Ask them to explain why they would pick it up. If they tell you they would pick it up because it belongs to them, place a paper clip next to the money. Tell them that both items belong to them, but that they may only pick up one. Most children will tell you they would pick up the money because it has value. So as not to lose it again, they will take care of it by securing it in a safe place (wallet, pocket, purse).

4. Explain to your children that the real value of money is not in the paper but in the ways money can be used to benefit themselves, others, or the environment.

5. Now ask for a volunteer from the group either to stand or lie down in the center of the circle (where the money was located).

6. Tell your children to imagine they are now looking down at themselves. Now ask, "As you look down at yourself, how do you determine value in yourself?" Ask them to share their ideas with their classmates.

7. Help your children to understand they have value because of who they are and what they can do to benefit themselves, others, and the environment (their community and society). Example: Ask your children if they would be willing to give up their sight (eyes) for the $100 bill. Most children will say no, because they value their sight and how it benefits them. Other elements of value might be their smile, personality characteristics, things they can do (skills), and so on.

8. Now ask a second question: "What are you doing to take care of what you value?" Example: I value my teeth for eating. I take care of my teeth through brushing and scheduled visits to the dentist.

Discussion

1. What is one thing you learned about yourself today?
2. Why is it important to care for what you value in yourself?

Lesson Variation

1. After discussing what gives a $100 bill value, have your children design their own bills. Let them determine the denomination and ask them to draw a picture of themselves (their faces) on it.
2. Now ask your children to share with their classmates the bills they have drawn and discuss what gives each of them value.

Scrap Lumber and the Candleholder

Objective: To help children understand that when they make something of themselves their value goes up.

Group Size: Classroom group

Time Required: 15–30 minutes

Materials: pieces of wood and wooden candleholder or some other object made of wood

Facilitator: The purpose of this activity is to help children recognize that life has value and that they can increase their value by creating a life of value as caregivers. Like pieces of wood, from the moment their lives begin, they have value. However, their value goes up when they make something of themselves, like wood made into a candleholder. You will be helping them to understand that being a caregiver first requires them to receive the care of others who will teach them how to care. Their value as caregivers will rise when they learn how to care for themselves, others, and the environment.

Process

1. Show two or three pieces of wood to your children and ask them if these pieces of wood have value, in that money is required to purchase wood.
2. Now show your children a candleholder or some object made from the wood shown earlier. Ask your children if the candleholder (object) has value (requiring money to purchase it).
3. Present the pieces of wood and the candleholder together and ask them which one has more value. Their response will favor probably the candleholder. If so, ask them why the candleholder has

more value. While their responses will vary, they will likely tell you that the candleholder has more value because of what the wood has become, a useful object.

4. Now ask your children how they are like pieces of wood and the candleholder. After some guessing, tell your children that like the pieces of wood, they have value because life has value and they are living human beings. Then explain to them that their value will rise (go up) when they make something of themselves (like the candleholder) and their lives.

5. Pieces of wood have potential, in that they can be transformed into objects of value. Human life has potential because, with the care and guidance of others, children can learn to become valued caregivers. Help children to explore skills, abilities, character traits, and hobbies they can develop and use to care for themselves, others, and the environment.

Discussion

1. Are you more like pieces of wood or the candleholder? Explain.
2. What are some things you can do to make something of yourself in a way that will increase your value?

Lesson Variation

1. Play the game, "I am a person who can . . ." Demonstrate this game for your children by telling them to fill in the blank with something they can do and then ask them to do it, if it is something they can demonstrate in class. For example: "I am a person who can *smile.*" Now smile.

2. If your children have difficulty identifying things they can do, help them to brainstorm a "can do" list of ideas and write them on the chalkboard. This list might include some of the following:
   • Read
   • Sing
   • Pay a compliment
   • Write
   • Draw

- Give myself a pat on the back
- Smile
- Add numbers.

Actions that cannot be demonstrated in class can be named, but not shown.

2. Help your children to understand that they are already making something of themselves by virtue of what they are learning and can do.

A Can of Cashews

Objectives

1. To help children understand that what gives them value and worth is on the *inside*.
2. To help children understand they can increase their value (net worth) by adding to their "can."

Group Size: Classroom group

Time Required: 30 to 60 minutes (one or two sessions)

Materials: can of cashews (corn, peas, etc.), can opener, paper towel, an empty container, empty vegetable cans without labels (one can per child), strips of white paper (the size of labels), scissors, magazines, crayons, paper

Facilitator: Help your children to recognize that much of what gives them value is on the inside. They can increase their value by filling up their "cans" and then list on their labels what is in their "can." In many ways, children are like cans of vegetables or cashews. It's what is on the inside that gives them value. Children can create what goes into their "cans" and then decide how to use what they have created to make a positive difference in their own lives and in the lives of others.

Process

1. Show your children an unopened can of cashews (corn, peas, etc.).
2. Ask your children to guess how much money the can is worth. After recording their guesses on the chalkboard, give them the correct amount.

3. Now open the can and dump the contents out on paper towels or into another container. Hold up the empty can and ask your children how much they will offer you for the can now. The amounts offered will be less than those given for the full can.

4. Ask your children to discuss why they are offering less for the can now. Most children will tell you the can is not worth as much now because the contents are gone. The contents gave the can more value.

5. Now ask children to tell you how they are like cans of produce (peas, nuts, etc.). Much of what gives them value is also on the inside.

6. Give each child an empty can and a strip of paper on which to create a label.

7. Brainstorm a list of things having value (hobbies; personality characteristics—kindness, courage, honesty, etc.; skills; ideas; knowledge; attitudes; sports; etc.) that might be found in their cans.

8. Have your children fill their cans with word descriptors, pictures from magazines, and objects that depict who they are on the inside.

9. When their cans are complete, have your children create labels from the provided strips of paper and ask them to attach them to their cans. Their labels will tell what gives them value.

10. Children can now sell their "cans" to the class. They are marketing themselves, by letting others know what gives them value. "I am a person of value because of my smile, I help with chores at home, I have these skills," and so on. Help your children to understand that being proud of themselves is different from bragging. Bragging involves putting someone else down—devaluing that person in order to make you feel better. An example of bragging is, "I am better at baseball than you."

Discussion

1. Who decides your value (worth) as a person? Help your children to understand that they are the ones who determine their own value. (Read "The Lady and the Vase" at the end of this section).

2. Help your children to understand that all people have value regardless of their differences, because all people have something to give (love, comfort, understanding, joy, etc.). Help your children to explore what gives their life value and what they have to give to themselves and others.

3. Read "The Balloon Salesman" at the end of this section. Have your children discuss the story's message and how that message relates to their own lives.

Lesson Variation

1. Help your children to understand that every day they learn something new, they are making something of themselves. Relate this concept to people in various careers who are required to learn information, skills, and new ways of doing things. They too are making something of themselves that adds to their value and worth (carpenters, teachers, firefighters, chefs, scientists, and so on). Discuss with your children that life has value and that this is demonstrated through a variety of careers that help to improve the quality of life for all people.

2. Ask your children, individually or in small groups, each to select a career and describe how that career demonstrates that life has value.

The Lady and the Vase

After the death of her husband, Mrs. Jones decided to get rid of all the junk in her attic. So she removed everything she could find of little value to her and spread the items out on her front lawn. She hooked up her garden hose and washed everything down, letting her belongings dry in the late morning sun.

She set up long tables and covered them with cloth, and then placed all the carefully marked items on the tables—two dollars for this and a dollar for that. Everything was marked low for a quick sale.

In the early afternoon, the sale began. Many people arrived, and the items went quickly. Mrs. Jones had one old vase left on the table. As she was about to close down the sale, an elderly gentleman approached the table and the lone vase. He picked up the vase, turned it around, and found "$2" written on masking tape. "Ma'am," he asked, "are you sure you want to sell this for two dollars?" Mrs. Jones looked at the vase, tore off the masking tape, and placed a new piece of tape, marked only one dollar. Then she handed it back to the man. He looked at it again and asked, "Are you sure you want to sell this for one dollar?" At this point, Mrs. Jones started to get angry, because she thought the old man was trying to get the vase for free. However, before she had time to confront the elderly gentleman, he said to her, "Don't you realize what you have here?" Mrs. Jones replied, "Yes, an old vase." To which he replied, "Ma'am, this is not only an old vase, but an antique vase worth somewhere around three hundred."

Mrs. Jones reached for the vase, clutched it to her chest, thanked the old man for his honesty, and ran into her house with the vase. She placed her treasure on the mantelpiece and now looks at it daily with kind eyes. She no longer hoses it down in the front yard but treats it with care, cleaning it daily with the finest of oils. This vase that was in the attic for so many years is now viewed as a treasure and has become the center of attention when people visit. Mrs. Jones cares for and cherishes the old vase as a thing of beauty.

1. What is the story about?
2. Is the vase that Mrs. Jones now has on her mantle the same old vase that she had in her attic?
3. What is now different about the vase?
4. In what way(s) are you like the vase (the vase in the attic and the vase on the mantle)?
5. People tend to take better care of those things they (fill in the blank). Explain.
6. If you view yourself as the vase in the attic, what are some things you can do to become the vase on the mantle?

The Balloon Salesman

Five-year-old Billy was visiting a summer circus in his hometown of Auburn, New York. He was born with one leg shorter than the other and used a wooden crutch to help him move about. As he was taking in all the sights at the circus, he noticed a rather tall old man wearing a long, dark coat and holding a large bunch of colored balloons. Every once in a while he would let one of the balloons go, and it would rise into the blue sky.

Very much taken up with what he had seen, Billy, with all the strength he could muster, propelled himself across the circus grounds to where the old man was standing. The little boy looked up into the great mass of balloons and found one that was different from all the others. This balloon was deformed.

Billy gave the old man's coat a tug. The old man looked down and their eyes met. At that moment, Billy pointed to the twisted balloon and said, " Mister, if you let that balloon go, will it go up, too?" Wanting to say something to the little boy that he would long remember, the old man paused for a moment before saying anything. Then he turned to the little boy and said, "Son, I want to tell you something about these balloons. It's not the size, shape, or color that makes them go up; it's what's inside that makes them go up."

Many years later, the little boy, all grown up, thought about the story and remembered the old man's words. How true they were, and how grateful he was for having received the old man's kind attention.

1. Why do you suppose the old man said that the size, shape, and color of the balloons were not important in giving the balloons a lift?
2. How are you like a balloon in the old man's bundle?
3. What gives you and your life lift?

The Chair Jump

Objectives

1. To help children recognize that sometimes people make choices that cause them to lose what they value.
2. To help children understand the importance of thinking before they jump (act).

Group Size: Classroom group
Time Required: 15 to 30 minutes
Materials: A steady chair

Facilitator: Impress upon your children that their lives have value. You will be helping them to understand that many children make choices that result in their losing what they value. This happens because some children do not think before they act and end up destroying something they value. In this activity, you will be using a "chair jump" exercise to illustrate the importance of pausing before you jump. When using this exercise, be sure to use a steady, four-legged chair. Place the chair on nonskid material, such as a large area rug. If a rug is not available, hold the chair for extra support. Select a child for the chair jump who follows directions and is a responsible student. At the conclusion of this experience, be sure to impress upon your children that all life choices have the potential for either helping or hurting themselves and others. They need to choose wisely and to think before they jump.

Process

1. Ask your children, "If you had a twenty-dollar bill, how many of you would be willing to cut it up into small pieces?" Most children will tell you that making that choice would destroy something they value.
2. Introduce the "chair jump" exercise. Select a child to come to the front of the room. Tell your class the selected child will do what we tell him/her to do. "Please stand on the seat of this chair facing the class. When the class counts to three (one-two-three), we want you to jump from the chair to the floor, landing on your feet." Following the first jump, instruct the child to stand on the chair once again. This time tell your volunteer to jump from the chair on the count of three and land on his/her face. Usually there is some laughter from the class and a long pause on the part of the volunteer.
3. Ask the class to answer why they think this person did not make the second jump. Help your children to recognize that their classmate *values* his/her face (health) and paused long enough to *think* about the harm that would come from making this jump.

Discussion

1. What do you value about yourself, (others, and the environment) that you would protect at all cost?

2. What are some choices people have made without thinking?

3. Sometimes people lose the very things they value most when they act before thinking. What are some of those losses (loss of life, friends, freedom, health, etc.)?

4. What is one thing you can do before you act? Think! "Will this choice *help* or *hurt* me, others, and the environment?"

Homework

1. Tell your children to read newspapers and magazine articles looking for choices children and adults have made that either resulted in their caring for what they valued or caused them to lose what they valued.

2. Present children with a number of life situations. Ask them to name choices they can make that will help them to protect what they value:

Life Situation	Choice	What I Value
crossing street	at cross walk	my life
riding in a car	wear seat belt	my life
meeting a new classmate	be friendly and introduce myself	making friends

What's in a Name?

Objective: To help children understand that families are proud of their last names because they value what they have created (positive reputations).

Group Size: Classroom group

Time Required: 15 to 30 minutes

Materials: None

Facilitator: Most people are proud of their family names. Their family names have been passed down from generation to generation along with family stories, good deeds, and valued family customs and rituals. Help children to recognize they too are contributing to their family's good names and will someday pass them on to others. A family name has value because people form impressions about all family members who share the same last name.

Process

1. Ask children to think of family names from history, the impressions they have of them, and how they were formed. Examples of some names to consider include: Lincoln, Nixon, Kennedy, Hitler, Disney, and Custer.
2. Have children gather information and pictures they would like to share that tell about their family and family history.
3. Ask children what they are doing and can do to bring value and honor to their family name. Have them brainstorm a number of ideas.
4. Ask children what they *would like others to think* when their family names are spoken.
5. Ask children to share things that family members sometimes do that *devalue* their family name:
   - Drive intoxicated
   - Take drugs
   - Hurt someone
   - Take things from others without asking
   - Disobey the law.

Discussion

1. Children can bring honor and value to their names every day. Help your children to explore ways in which they can do this at home, in school, on the playground, and with family members.
2. Tell your children that people from different cultures work very hard to bring honor to their names. Explore a few of these cultures (Chinese, Japanese, Native Americans, etc.).

SUGGESTED ACTIVITIES FOR THE WEEK

Language Arts and Reading

Have your children read stories, watch television and videos, listen to song lyrics, and discuss various sayings that demonstrate that life has value. Encourage your children to interview their parents, caregivers, and people from different careers (doctors, nurses, firefighters, police, religious leaders, emergency-response people, ambulance drivers, and so on) regarding their beliefs about the value of life and what motivates them to care. Encourage your children to write short stories, poems, and news articles about caring. Have them identify people in their homes, schools, and communities who have given much in support of others. Give your children an opportunity to tell their stories about such people through oral presentations. Have them write letters to these people (groups and organizations) expressing their gratitude for what they have done.

Math

Life has value and the value of life is recorded in the numbers. Explore with your children how numbers are used to help them to care and to be careful in lowering the risks they run. Identify places where numbers can be found and how these numbers are used to help people care and to be careful, because life has value. Numbers are found on houses, road signs, in motor vehicles, medical instruments, tires, food containers, bridges, in buildings, calendars, on meters, and so on. Numbers are used to save lives, conduct medical research, warn of danger, play games, solve problems, entertain, measure change, and support life. Have your children discuss what life would be like in the absence of numbers. In what ways do numbers demonstrate that life has value?

Science

The sciences are dedicated to improving the quality of life because life has value. Help your children to explore the various fields of science (medicine, space, biology, genetics, zoology, environmental science, geology, anatomy, nutrition, physics, and so on) and how they have contributed to our quality of life. The sciences exist to preserve life, improve the quality of life, extend life, and save lives. Explore with your children the various checks and balances that scientists must follow so as not to violate the sanctity of life while attempting to improve it. Help your children to understand that scientists must be careful while caring for themselves and others, because life has value.

Social Sciences

The social sciences focus on people and how people relate to each other. The goal is to understand people and to help them create caring and safe interpersonal environments, because life has value. Explore with your children the value that society places on all life forms, especially human life. Discuss with them how society communicates the value of life through the following entities:

- Meals on Wheels
- The U.S. Constitution
- Human shelters
- The Bill of Rights
- Health insurance
- The educational system
- Treatment centers (Health)
- The legal system.

Explore other groups and organizations that demonstrate that life has value.

Health and Physical Education

Health and physical education demonstrate that life has value by helping children to develop a wellness lifestyle. Children learn that the most effective health insurance comes from the caring and responsible choices they make in behalf of themselves and others. These courses teach children that their lives do have value and that they are responsible for managing their own good health. Explore with your children all that others have done for them in helping them to achieve a healthy lifestyle, and the caring choices they can make for themselves in support of the same.

Yes, life does have value. Our challenge is to help children value themselves and life so that they will be eager to receive what we have to give them, use what they have learned to invest in their own well-being, and pass on to future generations the best of what they have to give.

TIPS FOR CAREGIVERS

Your child's life has value. You certainly would not dispute this fact. However, it is equally important for children to value their own lives as

well. Children who value their lives will make caring choices to that effect. They will discover value in themselves and develop their potential
as givers and receivers of care. You play a most significant role in this
process, for it is in the home that children first discover their value as
loved and caring family members. This process begins at birth and continues into adulthood.

Many of the earlier activities in this chapter can be experienced at
home as well as in school. In addition to those experiences, the following
useful tips, fun ideas, and suggestions can help your children discover
value and worth in themselves and secure a place of value in the family:

1. Love your children. Help them to meet their physical and emotional needs.
2. Help your children to build trust in you by always being there for
   them and by providing them with a safe, secure, and predictable
   environment.
3. Provide your children with opportunities to do things for themselves commensurate with their age and stage of development.
4. Give your children opportunities to make mistakes and to try again.
5. Provide opportunities for your children to help out around the
   house:
   • Place their clothes in the hamper
   • Return their toys to the toy box after playing with them
   • Assist with household chores (wiping plastic dishes, dusting,
     emptying wastepaper baskets, and so on).
6. Heap praise, recognition, smiles, and kind words on your children
   for their caring contributions.
7. Help your children to become involved in meaningful family ac-
   tivities and to feel appreciated, loved, and respected as contribut-
   ing family members. Involve your children in:
   • Organizing and participating in family outings
   • Doing a variety of household jobs
   • Planning and contributing to family projects
   • Participating in family decision making
   • Volunteering, with you, in a variety of community service projects.
8. Teach your children a variety of life skills to include:
   • Goal setting
   • Decision making
   • Giving compliments

- Helping others
- Treating others with respect
- Using manners.

9. Help your children value themselves and see value in others by doing some of the following:
   - Place daily loving notes in your children's lunch boxes
   - Send them to school with hugs and kisses
   - Let them know how much you love them
   - Teach them to say "thank you," "please," and "may I"
   - When you interact with the public, point out to your children examples of people caring for each other
   - Help your children to identify acts of caring
   - Model various acts of caring for your children and have them practice what they have observed in you and others
   - Teach your children to smile and then have them give their smile to others
   - Teach your children simple acts of caring, like writing thank-you notes, opening doors for those in need, lending others a hand, raking leaves for the elderly, and so on; encourage them to share what they have with others
   - Create a caring word wall and add new words daily; challenge your children to use these words as often as possible
   - Explore with your children how they have benefited from the caring actions of others and that they too have a responsibility to care as well because life has value.

These ideas and activities are but a sample of the many things that you and your children can do together in helping them recognize that life has value. Involve your children in daily caring activities. Help them to understand and appreciate how loved and valued they are as caring family members. Help them to value themselves, what they have received, and what they can give to their friends, classmates, and community. They are becoming caring human beings and are taking their place in the circle of care, helping to enhance the quality of life for all people.

2

SEVEN CENTERS OF CARE

DEFINITION

Caring: Caring is a belief about how we should be with ourselves, others, and our environment. The Golden Rule is a belief statement that implies the importance of caring; it is a simply stated moral imperative that teaches us the value of treating others as we ourselves would like to be treated. Stated yet another way, caring represents "the activities, relationships, examples, and services offered young people which support their development and the attitudes, values, and behaviors that young people develop that in turn position them to value and participate in social service, social justice, and social change" (Pittman & Cahill 1992, 39).

BACKGROUND INFORMATION

Noddings (1992) stated that to care and be cared for are fundamental human needs the attainment of which give life purpose and meaning. Caring is the glue that connects us to ourselves, others, and the environment. "Without caring, individual human beings cannot thrive, communities become violent battlegrounds, the American democratic experiment must ultimately fail, and the planet will not be able to support life" (Lipsitz 1995, 65).

Many children in our nation, and their numbers are growing, are experiencing the devastating and cumulative effects of stress in their lives due to such causal factors as family poverty, homelessness, failing marriages, divorce, gang violence and vandalism, teen pregnancies, bullying, substance abuse, poor performance in school, dropping out of school, the constant threat of terrorism, and so on. If caring represents a belief about how we should be with ourselves, others, and our surroundings (environmental and societal), we must ask ourselves if we, as individuals and a nation, are doing what is ethically and morally right if we fail to care for our children. In response to this question, most people will come to similar conclusions, namely, that our society "needs to care for its children—to reduce violence, to respect honest work of every kind, to reward excellence at every level, to ensure a place for every child and emerging adult in the economic and social world, to produce people who can care competently for their own families and contribute effectively to their communities" (Noddings 1995a, 366).

Children, by nature, have the capacity to care and be careful (risk management) but often fail to make responsible, caring choices, because they themselves were not cared for by caring and responsible adults. The good news is that most children, even those who did not receive care, can become caring children and builders of caring communities when nurtured by people who do care.

Chapter 2 proceeds from the premise that caring children make caring choices to the extent that they understand the nature of care, are aware of the vast number of caring choices that are open to them, and are taught how to give and receive care. The pages that follow address these points.

The Nature of Care

Caring is multidimensional by definition, complicated and multifaceted in scope, and all-encompassing in practice. Caring counters violence, loneliness, exclusion, competition, and human suffering and increases thoughtfulness, cooperation, inclusion, responsibility, freedom, self-confidence, encouragement, and community building. Families, classrooms, and communities become caring and safe places when the people in them become responsible and generous givers and receivers of care (Worzbyt 1998).

Caring is more than a "warm fuzzy," although many people will tell you that it does feel good knowing in your head and heart that you are doing what is right (legally, ethically, and morally). Caring requires responsible action, although there are no magic formulas to follow in its execution. It is often described as a nurturing act, yet it can become a "gut wrenching" and painful experience in the context of responding to a moral dilemma with no easy solutions.

Caring is very much a time and energy-consuming act, the expression of which varies within individuals, between and among people, and from one situation to another. It has been described as a relational act (interpersonal), a virtue to be practiced, and a character trait to be cultivated. Lastly, caring has been described as a gratifying act of choice, a responsibility, a burden, a commitment to action, and a life-changing experience for givers and receivers of care.

Seven Centers of Care

As complicated and multifaceted as caring is, it can be reduced to a simple, yet powerful guiding principle: treat others as we ourselves would like to be treated. This comprehensive and helpful moral imperative focuses on matters of human caring in all its complexities, and it provides children and adults with an internal guidance system for making and receiving caring choices that are based on Right, Reality, and Responsibility.

Caring is the ultimate reality of life—to show concern, and to demonstrate interest in oneself, humankind, and the world (Worzbyt, O'Rourke, and Dandeneau 2003). Children who care revere life and living, respect all life forms, and make caring choices in support of themselves, others, and the planet. They understand risk and practice responsible risk-management strategies in their quest to care.

Caring, as I have described it, is central to all life decisions; it is at the core of what makes us human; and it gives meaning and purpose to life and living. It is what binds us together as people and helps us to meet our needs and wants as individuals in the context of supporting others and their right to do the same.

As important as caring is to ourselves, others, and the planet, it cannot be left to chance. The first job of home, school, and society is to "nurture the growth of competent, caring, loving, and loveable persons" (Noddings 1992, vii). I believe this goal can be best accomplished through a curriculum that develops intellectual competence while focusing on matters of human caring—a curriculum developed around human experiences that are shared by all children, a curriculum that gives meaning to their lives. The curriculum of which I speak addresses seven centers of care (Noddings 1992), which bring relevance to education by relating classroom learning to life and living, and by connecting homes, schools, and communities in a circle of care in which children learn how to give and receive care. The seven centers of care are (1) caring for self, (2) caring for intimate others, (3) caring for acquaintances and distant others, (4) caring for nonhuman animals, (5) caring for plants and the environment, (6) caring for the human-made world of objects and instruments, and (7) caring for ideas. For each center that has been identified, there are a variety of themes and activities that children can experience that will teach them how to care in the context of being careful.

The opportunities for caring are endless, and the themes to be explored in each caring center abound. Therefore, it is my intention to pique your interest in each center of care and challenge you to look beyond what I have written and discover for yourself the many possibilities that the seven centers of care hold for you and your children.

Caring for Self

Children are encouraged to explore the many different healthy and responsible ways in which they care for themselves (physically, emotionally, intellectually, and spiritually). Self-care strategies help children to make responsible caring choices in achieving a state of well-being and living with meaning and purpose.

Caring for self is a journey of self-discovery in which children develop a conscious awareness of themselves, others, and the world in which they live. They discover commonalities in human experiences and cultural differences and similarities. Most importantly, as children learn to care they discover their own self-worth (an unconditional love of self) and a love of life. They give priority to their own needs and happiness, and they love others as they love themselves.

What children learn at home, in school, and in their communities is what prepares them to care for themselves physically, emotionally, intellectually, and spiritually. The goal of self-care is to help children make caring choices that will enhance their own health and wellness.

Choosing Physical Health. We want children to understand what it means to be physically healthy and to make caring choices in support of a safe and healthy lifestyle. Children make physical caring choices when they:

- Become responsible consumers of health related information, services, and products
- Promote environmental practices that support good health
- Develop healthy eating habits
- Practice personal health care (grooming; eye, ear, and dental care; physical checkups; obtain adequate rest and sleep; and engage in daily exercise)
- Engage in responsible risk management in areas relating to injury prevention and safety
- Accept themselves physically
- Develop physical skills for playing games
- Practice daily relaxation strategies.

The goal of choosing physical health is to help children understand themselves, their environment, and the daily caring choices they can make to achieve physical well-being. Caring activities, like listening to music, reading, exercise, eating healthy meals, and positive self-talk represent caring choices that children can make to relax, have fun, and improve their physical sense of self.

Choosing Emotional Health. We want children to develop positive attitudes, collect valid and reliable information, and learn helpful skills that will enable them to understand and care for their personal and emotional needs. Children make emotional caring choices when they:

- Express their emotions appropriately and comfortably
- Practice effective communication skills (I-messages, listening, assertiveness)
- Use their personal strengths and characteristics to achieve their wants and needs

- Understand their dreams, hopes, and aspirations and strive to attain them
- Use character traits like self-discipline, patience, perseverance, kindness, honesty, and so on, as their sources of power to build life connections
- Possess emotional caring strengths like empathy, impulse control, anger management, and perspective taking
- Practice stress-management strategies like deep breathing, self-talk, counting to ten, and so on, when experiencing tension
- Utilize effective resistance skills in staying focused.

The goal of choosing emotional health is to help children understand the choices they can make in developing a positive emotional sense of self. Children who achieve emotional health feel good in their own skin. They accept personal responsibility for their own behaviors, express their feelings fully and openly, show concern for others, demonstrate empathy when others hurt, ask for help when needed, gracefully accept the help of others, demonstrate self-confidence and enthusiasm for life, manage stress responsibly, have clear values, pursue personal interests, and strive to self-improve in meeting life's challenges.

Choosing Intellectual Health. We want children to succeed in school and in life and to develop cognitive attributes that will enable them to think, reason, perceive reality as it is, and develop rational strategies for living. Children make intellectual caring choices when they:

- Set goals to achieve their needs and wants
- Solve problems and make decisions based on Right, Reality, and Responsibility
- Demonstrate a capacity for self-introspection and insightfulness regarding their conduct
- Accept responsibility for themselves and their actions
- Use thinking skills (observing, classifying, making assumptions, hypothesizing, giving feedback, interpreting, questioning, imagining, and predicting) and other proactive measures in lieu of merely reacting to life situations
- Apply a wide range of study skills and habits to improve learning
- Practice rational thinking strategies

- Possess an internal guidance system (legal, ethical, moral) that helps them to differentiate right from wrong.

Choosing Spiritual Health. We want children to understand their spiritual nature, to question their purpose for being, and to find meaning in their lives. As children experience the seven centers of care, they will understand the central role they play in life and living. They will discover their purpose for being—to give and receive care and to exercise caution when caring. They likewise will discover the pleasure and joy that comes from caring. *Caring is our purpose for being and what gives life pleasure and meaning.* When children understand this most significant life lesson, they will connect with the four life-defining questions presented in chapter 1, "My Life Has Value." The four questions are repeated here for emphasis.

1. What do I want to *be*?
2. What do I want to *do*?
3. What do I want to *have*?
4. What do I want to *give*?

The seven centers of care emphasize the importance of *becoming* caring human beings, learning to *do* what caring people do, *having* the caring attributes that caregivers acquire, and *giving* to self, others, and the planet all that caregivers have to give. This is how children develop a life of purpose and a life of meaning. The seven centers of care prepare children to take their rightful place in the circle of care, helping others to define their spiritual essence and live lives worth living.

Refer to handout 2.1 for help in caring for yourself.

Caring for Intimate Others

Children have a need to connect with important others in their lives. They are, by nature, social beings who seek meaningful relationships with parents, siblings, friends, classmates, teachers, and other caregivers. Caring is a relational process, in which there are caregivers and receivers of care. Caring begins when both the giver and receiver of care experience the transfer of care and acknowledge the transaction.

THINGS I CAN DO TO CARE FOR MYSELF

1. _____

2. _____

3. _____

4. _____

5. _____

6. _____

7. _____

8. _____

9. _____

10. _____

Handout 2.1

Consequently, children need to be taught how to give and receive care if a caring relationship is to be consummated.

Caring for intimate others (family and friends) is central to Erikson's psychosocial stages of development. Children first learn to trust, experience safety and security, and develop a sense of autonomy, initiative, and industry, leading to identity formation through their interactions and caring relationships with family and members of their inner circles. During these social exchanges, children learn what they must do to belong and establish places for themselves in their families, classrooms, schools, peer groups, social groups, clubs and organizations, and communities.

Children want to care for family and friends, and they succeed to the extent that they learn socially acceptable caring skills and use them in developing their relationships with others. Children are most successful in caring for intimate others when they exhibit the following characteristics (Worzbyt, O'Rourke, and Dandeneau 2003):

- Are respectful of others
- Form healthy relationships using caring social skills (manners, sharing, taking turns, giving compliments, and so on)
- Treat others fairly
- Resolve conflicts peacefully
- Cooperate with and encourage others
- Accept responsibility for their actions
- Have good perspective-taking and communication skills
- Are *we*-minded versus *I*-minded
- Have a positive sense of humor and are generally good-natured.

Healthful family relationships are formed when family members (Worzbyt, O'Rourke, and Dandeneau 2003):

- Spend time together
- Demonstrate respect for each other (listen, respect privacy, address each other caringly)
- Share ideas, concerns, successes, hurts, and feelings in caring ways
- Offer praise
- Give compliments
- Offer help

- Set rules for responsible behavior
- Use caring words and practice caring deeds in support of family solidarity.

Caring occurs between two people, but it also occurs in groups. Children are more likely to develop positive, caring relationships with intimate others when they understand the nature of groups, how they function, and the roles that various groups will play in their lives. Children must learn the benefits of groups, the forces that groups enact on their members and on themselves, how and why people form and join groups, what they stand to gain through group membership, and what caring choices they can make in support of the groups to which they belong. They must likewise be taught caring ways to acknowledge respectfully the receipt of care from family and friends, how to ask for care, and how to decline care gracefully and respectfully when it is not needed. Children will likewise require assistance in caring and identifying opportunities for giving and receiving care.

Children often have uneven exposure to caring. Some will be comfortable giving care but not receiving it, while for others the opposite will be true. Children typically are receivers of care. They do not have much practice in reaching out to other children, especially not to family and relatives. The goal of caring for intimate others is to give children what they need to build strong family and friendship connections using their caring assets.

Refer to handout 2.2 for help in caring for intimate others.

Caring for Acquaintances and Distant Others

It is often easier for children to care for family and friends (intimate others) than for people they don't know. After all, children have a vested interest in building positive family and friendship bonds. However, when it comes to acquaintances and distant others, giving and receiving care are likely to be given low priority. Consequently, caring for acquaintances and distant others often receives less attention than it should receive. Distance; cultural, racial, and ethnic differences; a lack of awareness; distrust; prejudice; fear; and misinformation are some of the factors that contribute to a reduction in the number and quality of

THINGS I CAN DO TO CARE FOR FAMILY AND FRIENDS

1. _____

2. _____

3. _____

4. _____

5. _____

6. _____

7. _____

8. _____

9. _____

10. _____

Handout 2.2

caring connections between and among people who are physically and psychologically removed from each other.

However, caring for people outside the inner circle is important if a global community of caring is to become a reality. Forming a caring commitment is critical, because however much we care for ourselves, we can never care enough in the absence of care from others. For example, children can make caring choices to protect the air around them, but if other people pollute the environment, these children will breathe unclean air. Therefore, children and adults must care beyond the inner circle if they and others are to experience a sense of safety, security, and belonging in a community that has a vested interest in all its members.

Caring for acquaintances and distant others is not only the right thing to do but absolutely necessary if we are to survive and thrive as a society and a global entity. While it is in our nature to care, human beings are also predisposed to engage in fight-or-flight behavior in the presence of perceived danger. People outside the inner circle, those whom we know least about, are thus easier to target, dehumanize, and hurt than those with whom we share close relationships. Consequently, racial tension, hate crimes, violence, highway rage, crimes against society, mistreatment of those who are different, and wars tend to involve acquaintances and distant others.

One of the greatest challenges facing children and adults today and tomorrow will be working and playing with people whom they know least about, in the spirit of developing a community of cooperation, inclusion, and caring. All people (children and adults) must strive to build a global family that addresses such societal issues as poverty, war, terrorism, racial and cultural unrest, environmental pollution, hunger, disease, waste of natural resources, and related challenges, issues that if not addressed will weaken us collectively and individually.

What, then, is the answer in helping all people, especially children, care for acquaintances and distant others? Where do we begin? Can we ever do enough to make a difference? There is no single answer or approach to helping children give and receive care beyond the inner circle. There are instead multiple approaches, the first of which is to help children become *aware* of their many acquaintances and people they don't know whose care they and their families have received without realizing it, care that has improved the quality of their lives.

We can help children to connect with care they have received by challenging them to become more aware of themselves, others, and their surroundings. For example, we can have children identify the names of authors whose books they have read and enjoyed; inventors and scientists who have improved the quality of their lives; news broadcasters and meteorologists who keep them informed and warn them of danger; automobile manufacturers who strive to build safer vehicles; local, state, national, and world organizations that fight poverty, clothe the poor, and raise money for medical research; and workers in their community who care for them and their families (police, firefighters, physicians and medical workers, and so on). Whether it is the clothes they wear, food they eat, books they read, games they play, chairs they use, the comfort of their home, or the telephones at their disposal, all that children have and use has been provided by acquaintances and distant others (people who care).

Children are enveloped in acts of care that they have received by the generosity of people they do not know. Collective caring (people giving and receiving care) is our life-support system, without which we could not survive. With awareness comes understanding and eventual action. First, children become *aware* of the caring acts of acquaintances and distant others. Next, they *understand* that there is more caring in this world than they ever thought possible. Lastly, they recognize that they too have much to give in support of those about whom they know little.

We must challenge children to look deep within themselves to discover what they have to give. We must likewise help children to understand that they are learning at home, in school, and in their religious training caring attitudes, skills, and attributes that are to be used in giving and receiving care. Some caring actions that children can use in caring for acquaintances and distant others are the following:

- Be polite (say "thank you," "please," "may I," etc.)
- Smile
- Offer help to others (helping hands)
- Give compliments
- Write letters and cards to people in nursing homes
- Thank people locally and nationally for caring.

The list of caring possibilities is endless, and those in need of care never ending. As children care and are cared for, they will appreciate the importance of being caring human beings. They will discover their purpose and the value of life and living.

A second approach to caring for acquaintances and distant others is to get to know others well. Mara Sapon-Shevin (1999), in her book *Because We Can Change the World*, offers many suggestions that children can use in learning about themselves and the multifaceted people about whom they know little. For example, children can interview people from different cultures, read books about those who are different from themselves, challenge stereotyping by learning the truth about issues of diversity, and work alongside acquaintances and distant others and learn from them.

Children live in a world where diversity abounds. Diversity exists in terms of age, gender, religion, ethnicity, physical appearance, mental capacity, interests, language, socioeconomic levels, health, and so on. People do differ from each other, and yet they share many things in common. All people are capable of giving and receiving care; what makes them unique is what they have to share. The goal of knowing others well is to learn to appreciate diversity and value what others have to give in building caring communities in which everyone belongs.

Games, activities, songs, literature, projects, and community service activities that foster cooperation and inclusion are encouraged, for they help children to connect with people of diversity. Caring for acquaintances and distant others can occur in shopping malls, on public transportation, at the beach, almost anywhere. It begins when children become sensitive to the needs of others and recognize that everyone has something to give and receive.

Can we ever do enough to make a difference in creating a caring world? That is a question I asked earlier in this chapter. I do not know the answer to this question. But I do know this: the old beachcomber, famous for throwing beached starfish back into the water, had it right when a stranger asked him how what he was doing could ever make a difference, given the vast number of starfish that needed his care. Looking down at his hand and the starfish in his grip, he was heard to say as he threw it back in to the water, "It makes a difference to this one." While our children will not be able to care for everyone in the world, they can help to change the world by caring for one person at a time.

Refer to handout 2.3 for help in caring for acquaintances and distant others.

THINGS I CAN DO TO HELP PEOPLE IN MY COMMUNITY, STATE, AND WORLD

1. _____

2. _____

3. _____

4. _____

5. _____

6. _____

7. _____

8. _____

9. _____

10. _____

Handout 2.3

Caring for Nonhuman Animals

Pets, domestic animals, and animals of the wild impact our lives daily. They are a source of pleasure, recreation, entertainment, clothing, food, protection; they offer care to those in need; and they play a major role in medical research. Animals are the subject of much discussion and debate with regard to how they are to be treated and how that treatment affects the balance of nature and the quality of life (theirs and ours).

Not a day goes by in which we are not reminded of the interdependence between animals and humankind. As each day passes, we learn more about how the quality of our lives is connected to the care that we provide nonhuman animals. Thus, caring for nonhuman animals is a center of care that touches all lives, especially children's lives.

Caring for domestic animals and pets is often the first experience that children have in developing a sense of compassion and responsibility with regard to the needs of those who cannot fully care for themselves. Despite this exposure, an estimated ten million pets are killed each year at humane societies and shelters (Noddings 1995b). Many pets are neglected, mistreated, abandoned, and suffer needlessly from physical cruelty and abuse.

Teaching children to care for pets and domestic animals often begins at home, and it extends to school, where children learn to love and respect their pets. They treat them with kindness and affection and receive the same in return. When children truly love their pets, they give care unconditionally and authentically, not out of duty or in obedience to parental demand.

Pets provide a source of companionship for the lonely, elderly, and medically fragile. They are a source of pleasure, love, and attention. They teach love, forgiveness, respect, kindness, and responsibility. Pets are trained to entertain, offer protection, and warn of danger. They help people to lower their anxiety, reduce high blood pressure, and manage stress. They offer independence and the freedom to live fuller lives to those with physical challenges. Pets give and receive care openly and unconditionally. They improve the quality of life for people and in return give them a reason for living.

Domestic animals also play major roles in children's lives. Children learn about the life cycle and how animals care for their young. They learn that animals are a source of food and clothing and that they are used in medical research in fighting disease and finding cures for devastating and life-threatening injuries.

Children are exposed to the use of animals in a variety of careers, including entertainment, law enforcement, farming, search and rescue, health care, transportation, and so on. They likewise learn that animals provide a source of employment for people who work as zookeepers, animal trainers, veterinarians, animal caretakers and groomers, pet store owners, and animal shelter providers.

Animals of the wild also deserve children's understanding and care. We want children to develop an understanding of the balance of nature and to become familiar with a variety of species and how they coexist together. We likewise want them to understand what happens when the balance of nature is upset and the role human beings can play in maintaining that balance. We want them to understand that some species of animal life have become extinct and that others are in danger of experiencing the same fate. We want children to know that they have much to give in caring for animals and to learn how to become involved in providing that care.

We want children to know of the ongoing conflicts and debates that call for their attention when caring people strive to strike the delicate balance between caring for animals and caring for people. Some areas of current conflict and debate relate to animal participation in medical research, the use of animals in the entertainment industry, animals raised for profit in the food and clothing business, and the killing of animals for sport (hunting).

Conflict and debate also arise when land and water usage decisions impact wildlife habitat. Logging, road construction, oil and gas drilling, mining, and housing construction are all industries that have had to be regulated in an attempt to achieve a reasonable balance in meeting the needs of animals and of people.

Our goal for children in caring for nonhuman animals is to help them to understand and appreciate the various roles that animals play in their lives. Children must learn about the importance of valuing animals and all that they provide, understanding extinction and its causes, learning to care and to be careful in the presence of animals, and understanding and becoming involved in the issues relating to maintaining a healthy balance between serving the needs of both animals and people.

Children can learn much about caring for nonhuman animals by reading stories about them, talking with people involved in animal protection and care, meeting representatives of animal-protection activist groups, discussing animal-protection laws with people who think they are too strict and negatively affect the quality of human life, visiting animal habitats, and becoming actively involved in animal care initiatives.

Refer to handout 2.4 for help in caring for nonhuman animals.

Caring for Plants and the Physical Environment

Caring for plants and the physical environment deserves attention, for both play a significant role in influencing our quality of life. We want children to understand that their life choices have far-reaching implications with repercussions beyond themselves. When plant life is threatened by noncaring choices, human life, and indeed, all life forms are threatened.

Plants filter the air that children and adults breathe and provide them with nourishment, medicine, clothing, and oxygen. Plants are a source of beauty; prevent soil erosion; add nutrients to the soil; and provide shelter, protection, and food for animal and fish life that helps to support human life. Plants provide people with employment, income, and a purpose for being. Plants decorate homes and places of employment and say "I love you" to those who receive them as gifts. Destroy plant life and we destroy nature's delicately balanced ecosystem, with effects we can only imagine.

If children are to appreciate truly the value of plants and all that they have to offer, they need opportunities to study them and make caring choices in their behalf. They need to experience the benefits that plant life has to offer and how those benefits can be so easily disrupted through careless acts arising out of ignorance or a disregard for others. Children need opportunities to care for their own gardens, greenhouses, and window boxes. They need to experience becoming caretakers and lovers of life. They need to experience all that plants have to give in support of their own lives.

Whether at home, in school, or in their communities, children can care for plants and learn about people in their communities who make a living and a life caring for plants. Farmers, foresters, plant shop owners, agriculturists, botanists, conservationists, horticulturalists, scientists,

THINGS I CAN DO TO CARE FOR NONHUMAN ANIMALS

1. _____

2. _____

3. _____

4. _____

5. _____

6. _____

7. _____

8. _____

9. _____

10. _____

Handout 2.4

medical researchers, and landscapers are just a few of the many people who care for plants in ways that will help plants to care for us.

Children can study different cultures, rituals, religions, ceremonies, and significant life events in which plants are used to promote caring. They can study the past and appreciate the value of plants through the ages. The growing of cotton and tobacco in the South greatly influenced people's lives and helped to shape the course of history. Crops and plants being raised today will likely influence our quality of life tomorrow.

As children learn about plants and how to care for them in ways that will help them to experience a better life today and tomorrow, they must likewise use caution in response to plant life that can cause them and others harm. Teaching children to recognize and to be careful around poisonous plants that can irritate the skin or even kill will be discussed in chapter 4.

With respect to environmental caring, children are encouraged to examine their surroundings and ask themselves what life would be like living in the presence of pollution (land, air, and water). Children likewise need to consider the extent to which their life choices contribute either to a polluted environment or an environmentally healthy planet. My contention is that many children are unaware of their daily choices, let alone how they impact the environment.

Human health (physical, emotional, social, intellectual, spiritual) is directly related to environmental health. What happens to one will affect the other. Children and adults depend on their environments for everything. Exercise, relaxation, social involvement, recreation, fun, and seeking oneness with nature are reasons that human beings give when they discuss their love of the environment. A healthy environment does for people what good soil, sun, and water do for plants. Neither can grow and remain healthy in the absence of a caring and nurturing environment.

When connecting with their environment, children must be challenged to participate in caring practices that will create and sustain a healthy environment, one that will be able to care for them. Teaching children how to get involved in promoting clean air, land, and water is a place to begin in addressing the many daily assaults upon our planet, our home.

Children must become aware of and concerned about the pollution of our land, water, and air; depletion of the ozone layer, which protects the earth from the sun's radiation; overpopulation; loss of forests; extinction of species and subspecies; dumping of toxic and nuclear waste; loss of natural habitats; and modifications in governmental regulations that once protected our national parks but now open them up to mining, lumbering, and drilling for gas and oil.

We want children to challenge decisions that are made in the name of progress but in reality may be motivated more by greed, competition, profit, and control by people striving to gain political or personal power at the expense of our environment. The challenges before our children are not easy ones, for responsible and caring decisions about the conflicts that exist among those who seek to use our natural resources and those who strive to protect them require full understanding of the issues.

Environmental caring is about striking a balance between protecting and maintaining a healthy environment, on one hand, and judiciously extracting natural resources that will improve our quality of life, on the other, without compromising what we set out to protect. In every instance, a caring balance needs to be achieved between what is good for people and what is good for the environment. This can never be an either/or choice—it takes people to create a caring environment, and it takes a caring environment to care for people.

Learning to care in the context of being careful requires all children to become sensitive and sensible decision makers (chapter 5). Caring choices that children make today will have far-reaching consequences for planet Earth and its inhabitants tomorrow.

Decisions regarding personal energy consumption, conservation of water, recycling, and participation in direct hands-on environmental activities should be a part of every child's education. Children must fully comprehend what they have to give in caring for their planet and in return what their planet has to give in caring for them. Children who enjoy quiet walks in the woods, hiking, camping, swimming, skiing (land and water), bird and animal watching, hunting, fishing, boating, or bicycling want these activities to continue. They recognize the pleasure that comes from enjoying their environment and the fact that their environment offers a lifetime of fun, relaxation, protection, medical resources, food, shelter, and so on.

What would life be like if all that children have come to count on from their environment was suddenly in jeopardy? We hope that no generation will have to face that prospect. However, because our precious resources (people, natural, economic) are limited and cannot be taken for granted, children must be taught that laws and personal rights mean little in preserving that which is good if people fail to commit themselves to living moderately, sensitively, responsibly, and with conviction in support of a caring environment.

See handout 2.5 for help in caring for plants and the environment.

Caring for the Human-Made World of Objects and Instruments

While the world of objects and instruments cannot care for people in a traditional sense, it can and does impact their lives in ways both caring and hurtful. The old adage, "What you care for will in turn care for you" is especially meaningful when considering the use of objects and instruments.

Children who care for their bicycles by making sure they are in good repair are likely to own bicycles that will care for them by operating in a mechanically safe manner. The same can be said for most objects and instruments that are designed to care for people. Consequently, if automobile seat belts, house smoke-detectors, books, pencils, and computers are cared for, they will most likely perform as expected and offer care in return.

Challenging children to examine the role that the human-made world of objects and instruments plays in their lives is important if they are to make caring choices regarding them. Children live in a world of technology. Because they have grown up with objects and instruments, children may be unaware of their presence, the significance they have in their lives, and the care they require in order to provide the care they were meant to offer. Traffic signal lights, cell phones, crosswalks, road signs and markings, chairs, computers, cameras, televisions, eating utensils, hand tools, guns, kitchen appliances, matches, carbon monoxide detectors, and swimming pools are but a few of the many objects and instruments in children's lives. While designed to improve the quality of life, these same objects and instruments have been misused or abused by some, resulting in personal injury, property damage, or death.

THINGS I CAN DO TO CARE FOR PLANTS AND THE ENVIRONMENT

Plants and Trees

1. _____

2. _____

3 _____

Water

1. _____

2. _____

3 _____

Animals, Including Birds

1. _____

2. _____

3. _____

(continued on the next page)

Handout 2.5

THINGS I CAN DO TO CARE FOR PLANTS AND THE ENVIRONMENT *(continued)*

Land

1. _____

2. _____

3. _____

Air

1. _____

2. _____

3. _____

State and National Parks

1. _____

2. _____

3. _____

Handout 2.5

Children require opportunities to explore their surroundings and the objects and instruments at their disposal. They need to understand their purpose, appreciate what they have to offer (caring potential), and know how to care for (proper storage and maintenance) and use them safely. In addition to proper care and usage, there is the importance of maintaining facilitative order (appropriate placement). Many objects and instruments need to be located usefully if they are to offer quality care. Toys need to be stored in centrally located toy boxes. First-aid kits and related safety devices must be strategically placed in areas of easy access if they are to offer the care for which they were intended. Chairs, lamps, tables, storage bins, and school supplies require proper placement to ensure safety, as well as ample work space and accessibility when completing work assignments.

Other topics worthy of exploration are the various uses of objects and instruments, the people who use them, and their historical perspectives. With respect to their use, objects and instruments play a major role in the remaining six centers of care. Children can have fun exploring how technology has impacted how they care for themselves, family and friends, acquaintances and distant others, nonhuman animals, plants and the environment, and ideas.

We want children to recognize the role that objects and instruments play in improving their quality of life. Children will enjoy exploring the impact that technology has on safety, transportation, health, recreation, creature comforts, and so on. Children are likewise encouraged to learn more about objects and instruments from the people who use them. This adventure takes children into a vast array of careers and career choices of a caring nature that require the use of technology in helping to facilitate that care. Doctors, nurses, farmers, construction workers, truck drivers, firefighters, police officers, teachers, chefs, and attorneys all use objects and instruments in their work as caregivers and receivers of care.

Objects and instruments also have a historical perspective as well. Children can have fun exploring why various objects and instruments were invented, who invented them, and when they first appeared as objects and instruments of care. Many improvements in technology have been made over the years that have changed how some objects and instruments look and are used. Many of these devices today are safer and more effective than their predecessors. Eyeglasses, telephones, electric lights, automobiles, airplanes, bicycles, and cameras have changed over the years, yet they continue to play roles in our lives today. We can help children learn about the past, connect with the present, and look to the future by explaining the importance that objects and instruments play in improving their quality of life.

Objects and instruments help to ensure safety, relieve human suffering and pain, enhance social relationships, foster spiritual connections through the use of symbols, facilitate ceremonial practices, and help us to understand better various cultures around the world. Despite all the good they provide, objects and instruments have caused human suffering, property damage, and death. Therefore, children must likewise be taught to be careful when sorting through the claims that have been made regarding the use of objects and instruments. False claims and fraudulent practices have resulted in harmful consequences to trusting and hopeful consumers. Caring must always be practiced in the context of being careful. More will be said about risk management and caring in chapter 5.

As children understand the human-made world of objects and instruments, they recognize that they live in a circle of care. Everything exists for a purpose. Objects and instruments are often the vehicles through which care is delivered and received. Books provide useful information, stimulating ideas, pose questions, cause reflection, offer suggestions, and move readers to action—all in the name of teaching children to care and to be careful. Objects and instruments must be understood, appreciated, evaluated, questioned, cared for, and used with care.

Making and using things is a part of children's nature. They need as much practice as we can provide in helping them to become active and responsible users of technology in caring for themselves, others, and the planet. Despite the potential pitfalls and dangers relating to caring, where would we be today without objects and instruments that have transported care into every domain of human life (Noddings 1992)?

Refer to handout 2.6 for help in caring for objects and instruments.

Caring for Ideas

Ideas about life and living gradually shape children's attitudes, beliefs, and values. Values translate into life goals and set the stage for how lives

THINGS I CAN DO TO CARE FOR OBJECTS AND INSTRUMENTS

Bicycle

1. _____

2. _____

3. _____

Automobile

1. _____

2. _____

3. _____

Fire and Smoke Detectors

1. _____

2. _____

3. _____

Books and Supplies

1. _____

2. _____

3. _____

Handout 2.6

are lived. As ideas germinate, they give life structure, meaning, and purpose. Ideas, once formulated, become an internal guidance system and provide the "how tos" for living a quality and purposeful life. Ideas help discern right from wrong, give life direction, and help establish paths of travel consistent with our values. When children identify with and care deeply for responsible and caring ideas through their actions, they care for themselves and everyone touched by the caring choices they make.

As important as ideas are to life and living, children must be challenged to examine their ideas and those that shape our nation and our world. Teachers, parents, caregivers, and community leaders have a responsibility to help children explore their ideas and formulate new ones relating to caring for themselves, family and friends, acquaintances and distant others, nonhuman animals, plants and the environment, and objects and instruments. Our goal must be one of helping children to cultivate responsible and caring ideas, ideas that will strengthen the balance of nature and enhance the quality of life.

By exploring a variety of caring ideas in the centers of care, children can identify those they wish to practice and eventually call their own. They can study moral imperatives, like the Golden Rule, and caring ideas governing fair play, kindness and compassion, proper etiquette, and good manners. They can also study ideas, past and present, and how those ideas have helped to shape their lives and the world order for good and otherwise.

With our guidance, children will understand that they live in a society shaped by convictions, values, and beliefs that are deeply held and provide a moral compass for living and making responsible and caring decisions. We want children to understand that people believe deeply in their ideas and that many have given their lives in support of their convictions.

Many of our nation's beliefs are captured in important documents and are reflected in our institutions, music, books, clothing, and so on. Our ideas about life and living literally permeate our way of life. The Gettysburg Address, the Preamble to the Constitution, and the Declaration of Independence are documents that define our values as a nation regarding the preservation of human rights. We have fought wars all over the globe in support of deeply held values, and we have created a democracy and a democratic form of government designed to preserve our ideas relating to the preservation of freedom.

In the absence of universally accepted sound ideas preserving the sanctity of life, our children would live in a virtueless society guided by what feels good rather than what is good for people and what helps them live together in harmony and in peace. Therefore, children must be taught to examine the soundness of their ideas and those shared by others. They must examine the risks associated with maintaining their ideas and passing them on to others. We want children to *notice* when something is not right—when caring and responsibility are at odds with ideas and behaviors that are designed to harm rather than help. We want them to have the *courage* to make a difference and stand up for what is right (legally, ethically, and morally). We want children to take action by employing strategies that will bring about change in preserving caring ideas like the Golden Rule (Sapon-Shevin 1999).

In a world driven by ideas, preserving the responsible and caring ones while challenging those that have the potential for doing harm gives voice to children's purpose in being—making caring choices and building caring communities. In so doing, they take their rightful place in the circle of care, giving, receiving, and passing on to others caring ideas of which we all can be proud. Refer to handout 2.7 for help in caring for ideas.

ROLE OF FACILITATOR

To care is to show concern and to demonstrate interest on behalf of oneself, others, and the environment. Your goal is to help children become caring human beings, capable self-managers, and builders of caring communities. Children are by nature caring people, and that nature must be nurtured by caring and loving adults.

Children are more likely to make caring and careful choices when they are taught how to care (give and receive) and to be careful (risk management). When caring children make caring choices, they experience a kinder and more compassionate society with fewer personal, social, political, economic, and environmental ills.

Teach children that giving and receiving care is what makes them human beings and gives their life purpose and meaning. Teach them that caring is at the heart of all life decisions and is the unifying force that brings and binds people together and supports them in their relationships with others.

IDEAS I CARE ABOUT: "WHY ARE THESE IDEAS WORTHY OF MY CARE?"

1. Be kind to others.

2. Always tell the truth.

3. Honesty is the best policy.

4. Brush your teeth after meals.

5. Say "thank you," "please," and "may I."

6. Change smoke detector batteries yearly and test monthly.

7. Practice the Golden Rule daily.

8. Exercise daily.

Handout 2.8

Throughout this chapter, you will be helping children to understand the nature of caring and what it means to be a caring person. You will help them to experience the relevance and purpose of classroom instruction and how it relates to caring, life, and living. This is accomplished by introducing children to the seven centers of care. These centers encompass the vast majority of all life choices that children will make during their lifetime. They are restated here for emphasis:

- Caring for self (physical, emotional, intellectual, spiritual)
- Caring for intimate others (family and friends)
- Caring for acquaintances and distant others
- Caring for nonhuman animals (domestic and wild)
- Caring for plants and the environment
- Caring for the human-made world of objects and instruments
- Caring for ideas (guiding principles).

These centers of care, when linked with academic instruction, help to foster a coherent curriculum that facilitates understanding and brings relevance and purpose to learning by focusing on matters of care. Caring is central to every academic domain and gives education its purpose— namely, to produce competent, loving, and loveable people who become citizens of the world and builders of caring communities.

Rather than focus on traditional subjects as isolated units of content, you can help to make children's education more meaningful and relevant to their lives by creating an integrated curriculum around universal human experiences (the seven centers of care). This approach will help children identify with the caring attitudes, ideas, and skills they have learned and learn how to use them in support of humankind.

Help your children to understand that what they care for will care for them. When children care for their bodies, their bodies will care for them, by performing in a healthy manner. When children care for plants and the environment, they will be there to care for them and others, by way of a balanced ecosystem that supports life. When children care for family and friends they increase the likelihood that they will be treated in kind by them. The seven centers of care require care before they can return the care they were meant to provide.

Teach your children the Golden Rule, how it works, and the value of practicing it daily. Help them to understand that caring people make caring choices and that they were meant to give and receive care. Teach them that caring is what gives life purpose and meaning, that it is one of their greatest and most precious gifts to the world. Teach your children how to receive and appreciate the care given to them by others, how to ask for care when needed, and how to respectfully decline care when it is not desired. Teach your children that care is a reciprocal process in which givers and receivers of care acknowledge and appreciate what the other has done in building a caring relationship. Teach your children that they have an increased responsibility when offering care to those who are unable to care for themselves. People who are ill, the elderly, the very young, those with physical or mental challenges, and animals require the full attention of caregivers who value life and who seek to help others live a quality life.

This chapter has been about caring in the seven centers of care. It has also been about helping children to rise to their full potential as givers and receivers of care. What follows is a variety of activities that will help you to help your children experience what they were meant to *be,* caring human beings who value life and the planet that sustains it. Have fun helping your children develop a caring spirit and find their places in the circle of care.

BENEFITS TO CHILDREN

Children who care:

- Use their caring attitudes, ideas, and skills to make caring choices
- Make caring choices in the seven centers of care
- Give, receive, request, and decline care in a caring manner.

PITFALLS TO CHILDREN

Children who do not care:

- Hurt, and sometimes hurt others
- Fail to recognize or appreciate the virtues of caring
- Find it difficult to develop and maintain caring connections.

ACTIVITIES

Things That I Do to Care for Me

Objective: To help children examine caring choices they can make for themselves.

Group Size: Classroom group

Time Required: 15 to 30 minutes

Materials: Sentence completion sheet

Facilitator: This activity is designed to help children connect with the many daily self-caring choices they can make. After your children finish their sentence completion sheets, have them sit in a circle with you and share their ideas.

Process

1. Give each child a sentence completion sheet (handout 2.8).
2. Tell your children to write a caring response for each sentence stem. Ask children who have a difficult time expressing themselves in writing to think of a response and then write a few words to help them to remember what they want to say.
3. Have your children sit in a circle and share their responses to selected sentence completion items. Help your children to recognize that self-caring can be expressed in many ways.
4. Ask your children to share some self-care choices they have made today, this week:
   - Brushing teeth
   - Bathing
   - Eating a balanced breakfast
   - Saying nice things to themselves
   - Saying no to things that could hurt them
   - Wearing a bicycle helmet.

Discussion

1. Help your children understand that they make many choices during a day. Tell them that it is important for them to make caring choices for themselves.

SELF-CARE SENTENCE COMPLETION

1. A positive way that I take care of myself is: _____

_____

2. When riding in a car, I: _____

_____

3. When I have a headache, I: _____

_____

4. When I get home from school, I: _____

_____

5. When walking on the road, I: _____

_____

6. When riding my bicycle, I: _____

_____

7. To relax, I: _____

_____

(continued on next page)

Handout 2.8

SELF-CARE SENTENCE COMPLETION (*continued*)

8. To have more energy, I: _____

_____

9. When I get upset or angry, I: _____

_____

10. To help me feel better about myself when I am down, I: _____

_____

11. When I have a problem, I: _____

_____

12. When someone tries to get me to do something I think is wrong, I:

_____

_____

13. To take care of my body, I: _____

_____

14. An object/instrument that I use that helps me to take care of myself is: _____

_____

Handout 2.8

2. Brainstorm different activities and life situations that children experience everyday.
3. Write them on the chalkboard.
4. Tell your children to state caring choices they can make for themselves for each life situation item listed. Sample items might include:
   • Playing outside in the winter—wearing warm coat and hat
   • Walking along a roadway—walking along the left-hand side of the road facing oncoming traffic
   • Visiting their doctors—asking the doctors questions about good health
   • Riding in a motor vehicle—
   • Grocery shopping with their families—
   • Playing baseball—

Homework

1. Have your children keep a daily diary of all the things they do. Have them divide each page in half with a vertical line. On the left side have them write life experiences and on the right side a self-care choice for each life experience listed.
2. Alternatively, you could have your children write down self-caring choices they observe people make in the mall, in stories they read, in television programs they watch, and self-care choices made by people whom they study in language arts, science, social studies, etc.

Self-Affirmations

Objective: To teach children a self-care technique called self-affirmation.
Group Size: Classroom group
Time Required: 15 minutes
Materials: None
Facilitator: Children are inclined by nature to engage in self-talk while participating in a life experience and continue to do so after the experience has been completed. Sometimes the self-talk is negative, in which children engage in name-calling, put-downs, and telling themselves hurtful things. The end result is diminished feelings

about self, a reduced energy level, loss of confidence, and an eventual retreat from new activities. Help children recognize their successes and treat themselves with kind eyes.

Process

1. Explain to your children that they are going to learn a valuable self-care technique called self-affirmation, or giving yourself praise and recognition for your accomplishments. Tell your children that no matter how poorly they may think they have done, they can always find something positive and then vow to find ways to self-improve. For example, trying something new for the first time, even if success is not attained, is worthy of a self-affirmation.
   a. Identify something you have done of which you feel proud. Write it on paper.
   b. Decide how you feel (example: pleased, happy, overjoyed, courageous, helpful, kind).
   c. State how you feel and what you have done. Give yourself a pat on the back. For example, "I feel happy because I raised my hand in class even though I was scared. I deserve a pat on the back."
2. Ask your children to practice giving themselves self-affirmations. Guide your class through each step. Some children will have trouble with the first part of this (part a).
   a. Some caring things children have accomplished are:
      - Being in class
      - Making friends
      - Raising their hands in class
      - Opening a door for someone
      - Coming to school on time
      - Returning a lost item
      - Listening to the teacher
      - Following directions.

   Encourage your children to select a caring action from the chalkboard if they can't think of one.
   b. "I feel (fill in the blank)."
   c. "I feel (fill in the blank) because I (fill in the blank). I deserve a pat on the back."

3. After your children learn how to give self-affirmations, you can take self-affirmation breaks throughout the day. Do them verbally at first; later in the year they can be done silently.

Discussion

1. Help your children to recognize that they do many positive things all day long. While they do many positive things, their successes may go unnoticed by others. However, they can learn to feel good about themselves and treat themselves with kindness through caring self-affirmations.
2. Ask your children to discuss how they feel about self-affirmations. Is it a good idea?
3. Help your children to identify times and places when they can use self-affirmations.

Homework

Have your children interview parents, teachers, friends, and relatives about things they have done for which they are proud. Ask your children to identify ways in which these people reward themselves (gave self-affirmations, bought something nice for themselves, took some time off, gave themselves a treat—bath, read a book, etc.). Note: As children participate in self-affirmations, they will become more self-aware of their positive qualities and behaviors.

Random and Planned Acts of Caring

Objectives

1. To help children explain caring choices in the seven centers of care
2. To help children understand that what they care for will in turn care for them.

Group Size: Classroom group and small work groups
Time Required: 30 to 45 minutes
Materials: Seven worksheets (one worksheet for each center of care)

Facilitator: While most children understand what it means to care for themselves, family, and friends, few children have given thought as to ways in which they can care for distant others, objects and instruments, their environment, or ideas. Help your children to recognize that random and planned acts of caring benefit not only those receiving the care but those giving it as well. For example, when children care for their bicycles (objects and instruments) by keeping them in good repair, their bicycles will not only last longer but will help to keep them safe in return. In the activity that follows, children will be divided into seven separate groups. Each group will be assigned a center of care and will brainstorm examples of caring for that category. After the brainstorming session is over, the various groups can share their ideas.

Process

1. Divide your class into seven groups.
2. Assign each group a different center of care.
3. Give each group a brainstorming worksheet for their center of care.
4. In order to help your children begin their brainstorming assignment, work together as a class brainstorming a few ideas for each center of care.
5. Children in the *Caring for Ideas* group will have a completed worksheet. Their task will be to state reasons why they believe these ideas are helpful and caring ideas to practice.
6. What follows are some caring suggestions for each caring center:
   a. Things I Can Do to Care for Myself (see handout 2.1 on pg. 34)
      - Take a bath
      - Brush my teeth
      - Exercise.
   b. Things I Can Do to Care for My Family and Friends (see handout 2.2 on pg. 37)
      - Give them compliments
      - Listen to them
      - Tell them that I love them
      - Share toys
      - Take turns
      - Help with chores
      - Make sure they wear seat belts.

c. Things I Can Do to Help People in My Community/State and World (see handout 2.3 on pg. 41)
- Rake leaves for older people
- Read to people whose eyes are failing
- Wash cars
- Shovel snow
- Join community fund raisers to help people in need.

d. Things I Can Do to Care for Nonhuman Animals (see handout 2.4 on pg. 45)
- Clean cages
- Provide water
- Feed
- Provide shelter
- Veterinary visits
- Volunteer at the animal shelter
- Follow hunting guidelines.

e. Things I Can Do to Care for My Environment—Brainstorm ideas for various environmental categories (see handout 2.5 on pp. 49–50)
- Plants/trees
- Animals
- Air
- Water
- Land.

f. Things I Can Do to Care for Objects and Instruments— Brainstorm ideas for each category (see handout 2.6 on pg. 53)
- Bicycle
- Electrical appliances
- Automobile
- Skateboard
- Playground equipment
- My school books and supplies
- Fire and smoke alarms.

g. Ideas Worthy of My Care—Ask your children why they think each idea is worthy of their care (see handout 2.7 on pg. 56)
- Be kind to others
- Always tell the truth
- Honesty is the best policy

- Brush your teeth after meals
- Say "thank you," "please," and "may I"
- Change smoke detector batteries yearly and test monthly
- Practice the Golden Rule daily
- Exercise daily.

7. After five to ten minutes of brainstorming, ask each group to share some of its ideas with the class.

Discussion

1. Help your children to understand that what they care for will care for them. Illustrate this point using a few of their examples from each center of care.
2. Help your children to understand that they make many choices in a day. Every choice they make can either be a caring choice or a harmful one. Help your children to make caring choices in each center of care.
3. Ask your children how it feels to care and to be cared for.
4. If caring feels so good and is helpful to so many people, ask your children why they believe more caring choices are not being made by everyone.
5. Ask your children what they can do to make more caring choices than they ever thought possible.

Homework

Have your children observe caring in each center of care. Ask them to record their observations and to share them with the class. Have your children make "caring coupons" or "caring recognition awards" and mail them to people who care. Have your children brainstorm and carry out acts of caring at home, in school, and in their community. See figure 2.1 for a sample of a caring recognition award, and handouts 2.1 to 2.7.

Caring Strategies

Objectives

1. To help children *ask* for help appropriately
2. To help children *offer* help respectfully

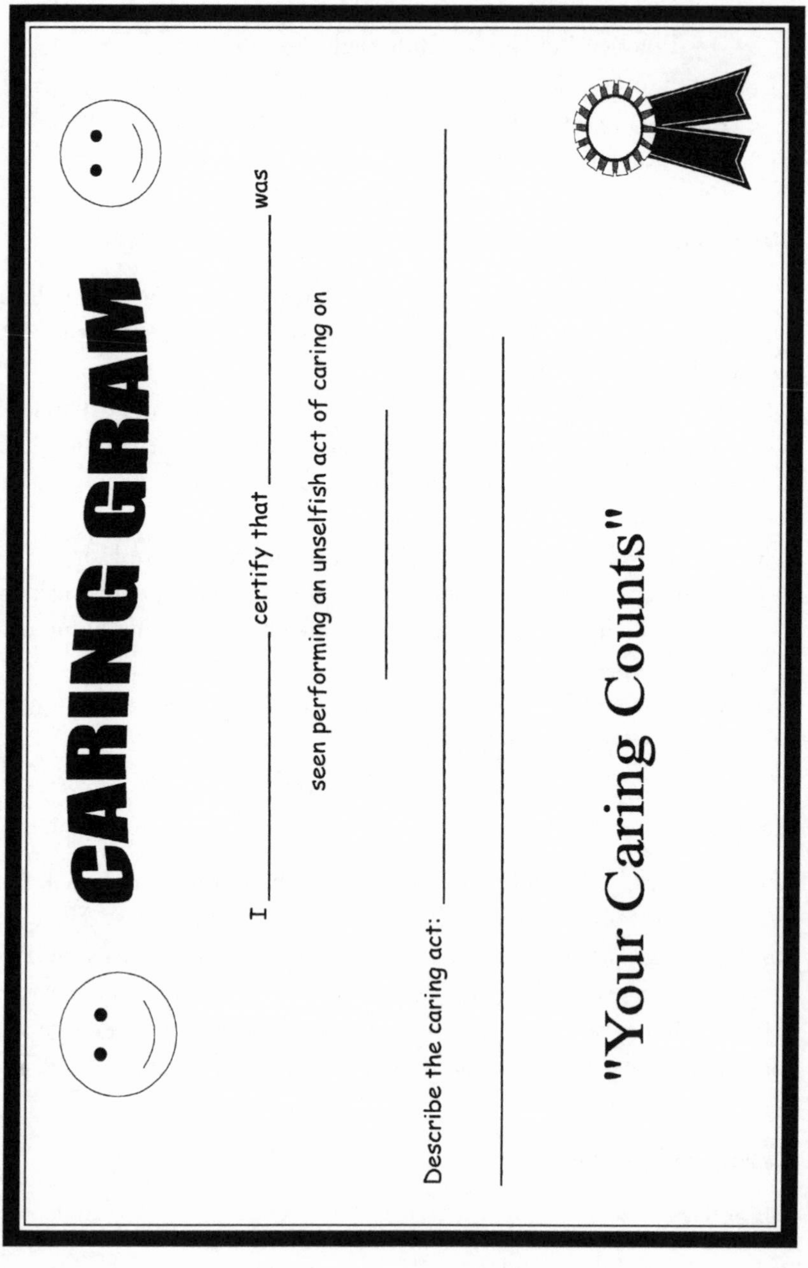

CARING GRAM

I _____ certify that _____ was
seen performing an unselfish act of caring on
_____

Describe the caring act: _____
_____

"Your Caring Counts"

Figure 2.1. Sample caring recognition award.

3. To help children *accept* help graciously
4. To help children *decline* help kindly.

Group Size: Classroom group
Time Required: 30 to 45 minute
Materials: handout 2.9 (HELP)
Facilitator: Explain to your children that all people need help from time to time. You might need help but not know how to ask for it appropriately. You might want to offer help but don't know how to offer it respectfully. At times you may be offered help but are not sure how to accept it graciously. At other times, you may be offered help you do not need and are not sure how to decline it kindly. This activity will teach you four caring strategies that you can use to ask for, offer, accept, and decline help. We will be practicing these strategies together so that you will be able to use them when they are needed (Shapon-Shevin 1999).

Process

1. Give each child a copy of handout 2.9.
2. Teach each caring strategy separately, using the guidelines in the handout.
3. Discuss *Asking for Help Appropriately* with your children.
4. Ask for volunteers to demonstrate Situation 1. Do this role play in front of the class.
5. Ask your children to work with a partner in role-playing Situations 2 and 3. Children are to take turns *asking* for help appropriately.
6. Role-play Situation 4 in the large group.
7. Teach the three remaining "help" strategies by repeating steps three through six.
8. After your children have practiced the four "help" strategies, create and conduct two-person role plays using the following strategy combinations:
   a. Asking for help—offering help
   b. Offering help—accepting help
   c. Offering help—declining help.

Discussion

1. Ask your children what it was like for them to ask, offer, accept, and decline help. Have them share which strategies were easy to do and which ones were more difficult!
2. Ask your children how they felt when their offer for help was declined. The declining of help in a caring manner is easier to accept than noncaring rejection.
3. Ask your children to discuss the following questions:
   a. When is it acceptable to ask for help?
   b. When is it appropriate to offer help?
   c. When is it okay to accept the help of others?
   d. When is it okay to decline the help of others?
   e. Share a time when you used one of these caring strategies.
   f. Discuss how the four "caring" strategies can be used at home and at school.

   Why is it important for you to acknowledge the help of others in caring ways even if you decline the help offered?

Homework

1. Ask children to create their own role play situations using the four "caring" strategies. Have them record their ideas on three-by-five-inch index cards and role-play their ideas in class.
2. Ask children to observe examples of the four "caring" strategies. Encourage them to find examples of their use in newspapers, books, movies, at home, at the mall, on the playground, and so on.
3. Ask your children to select and practice one of the four "caring" strategies during the week. Have them write what they did so it can be shared in class.

See handout 2.9.

Doing the Right Thing

Objective

1. To help children increase their awareness of issues and problems in the world relating to the seven centers of care

HELP

Directions: Today you will learn how to:

1. Ask for help appropriately
2. Offer help respectfully
3. Accept help graciously
4. Decline help kindly.

Your teacher will help you to understand and practice four ways to care using the examples on this page.

Asking for Help Appropriately

How many times have you wanted to ask for help but didn't know how to do it or were afraid to ask? This has happened to most of us. Here are a few suggestions that you can use to get the help you need. "I would appreciate it if you would help me with (fill in the blank)." "I am having trouble with (fill in the blank). Would you please help me?" "I don't know how to (fill in the blank). Would you be kind enough to help me?"

Practice saying these phrases to yourself. Share with your teacher other caring ways to ask for help when help is needed.

Situation 1: You have your arm in a sling and need help carrying your lunch tray. What do you say?

Situation 2: You go to the store to buy a book. You cannot find the book you want. What do you say?

Situation 3: You are feeling alone and would like a hug from a family member. What do you say?

Situation 4: On your way home from school, you notice that a stop sign is lying on the ground. You are afraid that there might be an accident at this intersection. You try to put the sign up but can't get it to remain standing. Who will you ask for help, and what will you say?

Offering Help Respectfully

How many times have you wanted to offer someone help, but did not know how to do it? Well, here are a few ideas. "Can I help you with (fill

(continued on the next page)

HELP (continued)

in the blank)?" "May I offer you a hand?" "If you would like some help with (fill in the blank) let me know. I will be pleased to help." Practice saying these phrases to yourself. Share with your teacher other caring ways to offer help respectfully.

Situation 1: You see one of your classmates loaded down with books. She/he needs help opening the door. What do you say and do?

Situation 2: Susan is sitting at her desk with her head down and whispering to herself, "I can't get this math problem." You hear her words. What do you say and do? Do you show her how to do the problem, or do you do it for her? Explain!

Situation 3: You are on the playground and see a little boy (first grade) fall off the slide. He is crying but is not injured. What do you say and do?

Situation 4: You overhear two parents talking to each other while at a school sports event. They are looking for their son. You know where he is. What do you say and do?

Accepting Help Graciously

Accepting the help of other people is not always an easy thing to do, but sometimes help is needed. Learning to accept help in a gracious manner is a way that you can care for the person helping you while receiving the help you need. Here are a few suggestions that you can try when accepting the help of others. "Thank you for helping me, I really appreciate it." "You are so kind to offer me your help." "I am glad that you noticed that I needed help with (fill in the blank). Thanks." Practice saying these phrases to yourself. Share with your teacher other caring suggestions for accepting the help of others graciously.

Situation 1: You are helping a family member carry groceries to the car. Just as you are about to drop one of the bags, a store employee rushes to your assistance. What do you say to this person?

Situation 2: Your best friend's mother is going to drive both of you to school. You get into the car and start to buckle up, but you are having trouble fastening the buckle. Your friend, seeing that you need help, offers to help you. What do you say to your friend?

(continued on the next page)

HELP (*continued*)

Situation 3: You are at the mall and need to call home. You discover that you don't have your cell phone. A friend offers you the use of his/her phone. What do you say to your friend?

Situation 4: You are wrapping a gift for a family member. You discover that you need help holding the paper, cutting the tape, and tying the bow. Your teacher sees you struggling with this task and offers to lend a helping hand. What do you say to your teacher?

Declining Help Kindly

Have you ever been in a situation where you wanted to do something all by yourself when someone offers you help? You do not want to hurt this person's feelings, but you do not want their help. This awkward situation can be avoided if you know how to decline help kindly. Here are a few ideas. "No thank you. I want to see if I can do this without help." "Thank you for asking, but I think I can do this myself." "Your kindness is appreciated, but this is something I want to do." Practice saying these phrases to yourself. Share with your teacher other caring suggestions for declining help kindly.

Situation 1: You are struggling with a math problem. Your friend approaches you and offers to help. You want to see if you can do this math problem on your own. What do you tell your friend?

Situation 2: Your mother (family member) always lays out the clothes you will wear to school. You want to select your own clothes. What can you say to your mother (family member)?

Situation 3: Bill has his own way of studying for a test. He thinks his way is best. You and Bill decide to study together. Bill wants you to prepare for the exam the same way that he prepares. You want to use your own method. What can you say to Bill?

Situation 4: You are playing baseball. Your coach has been helping you to catch fly balls. You are doing better but are still having some difficulty. You think that with practice you will continue to improve. You are approached by another player who offers to show you how to catch fly balls. You want to continue practicing what your coach has been teaching you. What do you say to this player?

Handout 2.9

2. To help children take a stand regarding their beliefs
3. To help children act on their convictions.

Group Size: Classroom group
Materials: None
Facilitator: Explain to your children the importance of learning about community and global problems and issues. Help them to understand that caring begins when they notice that not everyone makes responsible, caring choices. Unfair practices, injustices, and inequities exist among people and need to be changed. Also, our planet is sometimes lacking in care, resulting in harm to the land, air, and water. Tell children that it is important for them to *notice* both caring and harmful choices being made in the seven centers of care. When they notice problems and issues at home, in school, in their community, and around the world, they will *understand* that more caring choices need to be made and the harmful ones stopped. Understanding leads to *action* for those who know what to do and have the courage to act. Explain to them that courage means doing what you must, even in the face of fear. Caring and courageous people stand up for what is right in the seven centers of care despite the challenges they may face along the way.

Process

1. Explore each center of care with your children. Help them to notice the helpful and harmful choices being made by themselves and others. This can be accomplished by helping your children to understand that not all people are treated fairly, because of their race, age (young and old), gender, social status, religious affiliation, disabilities (physical and mental), and so on. Also, help them to see some of the inequities in society that impact the way people are treated in areas related to poverty, homelessness, hunger, abuse (physical, mental, sexual), and so on.
2. As you help your children to notice some of the hurtful choices people make in the seven centers of care, also help them to un-

derstand that many people, when they notice that things are not right, will work hard to bring about change. Explore with your children the names of people (children and adults) who have helped to bring about positive change in the seven centers of care and what they did to make change happen.

3. Explore with your children skills they *have* and things they can *do* to make their home, school, community, and world more caring places. Some examples of skills that they have are the following:
   - Talking to other people
   - Asking questions
   - Writing letters
   - Reading and gathering information
   - Decision making
   - Goal setting.

   Some examples of things that children can do to improve caring in the seven centers are:
   - Write letters to people thanking them for taking a stand doing (fill in the blank)
   - Gather information about an endangered species and learn what can be done to help address this problem
   - Advocate on behalf of clean parks and recreation sites
   - Increase caring classroom choices while reducing and stopping hurtful choices (name calling, racist joke telling, bullying, and discriminatory practices).

4. Discuss with your children what it means "to do the right thing." People who "do the right things" use Right, Reality, and Responsibility to guide their actions. Ask them to identify people (and their actions) who they believe have done the "right thing." Children can use literature, movies, newspaper articles, and their own personal observations in identifying people who have acted courageously and with conviction in doing what is right.

5. Explain to your children that "doing the right thing" is a choice they too can make. Have them share with each other their own acts of courage as well as the courageous acts of other children doing what is right.

Discussion

1. Ask your children to discuss what "doing the right thing" means to them.
2. Ask your children to explain the meaning of courage and to provide some examples of courage.
3. Ask your children to share how "doing the right thing" sometimes takes courage. Discuss people in history and the present day who have exhibited courage "doing the right thing."
4. Have your children discuss some examples of "doing the right thing" and how these examples relate to caring.
5. Ask your children if they believe we need more people "doing the right thing" and their reasons for thinking this way. Ask them to consider what life (home, school, community, and global) would be like if "doing the right thing" was no longer thought to be important.

Homework

1. Have your children interview police, teachers, religious leaders, parents, community leaders, and others regarding their thoughts on "doing the right thing." Children can write reports based on their interviews and share what they have written with class members.
2. Have your children keep a "doing the right thing" notebook. Every time they "do the right thing," they are to record what they did in their notebook. These acts of caring can be placed in a class notebook so that children can appreciate individual acts of caring and what many people can accomplish when they choose to "do the right thing."

SUGGESTED ACTIVITIES FOR THE WEEK

Language Arts and Reading

Have children read books and articles, give book reports, make speeches, and write papers on various aspects of caring (caring for self, family and friends, distant others, nonhuman animals, plants and the environment, objects and instruments, and ideas). Help children become more aware of the importance of caring and how the written and spoken word can enhance or destroy caring. Children can study written and spoken words in advertising, movies and plays, politics, sales, newspapers, and cards. Help them understand the power of literacy and ways they can use words to benefit humankind.

Math

We live in a world of numbers. Numbers can be used to help people make caring choices, enhance the quality of life, and save lives. People can learn much about themselves through numbers and communicate with others in helpful ways using numbers. Help children understand how their health and wellness is determined by numbers. Have children brainstorm ways that numbers are used in the seven centers of care and how they benefit from these numbers. Page numbers; clothing, hat, and shoe sizes; weight; height; blood pressure; calorie calculations; heart rate; liquid measurement; nail lengths; yards of concrete; days of the week; months in a year; seconds; minutes; addresses; phone and fax numbers; social security numbers; birth dates; and mathematical computations used in digging tunnels, building bridges, and designing ships and aircraft are examples of numbers that people use to care and to be careful in the seven centers of care.

Science

Science helps people to better care for themselves, others, and the environment. Help children explore the various sciences and the caring contributions they have made. However, for every caring act that science provides, there is the potential for harm. Help children identify examples of negative side effects that can come from science and how science works to reduce them. Help children identify some of the caring strengths (assets/skills) they have learned in their various science units. Ask your children how many of them are using these caring skills to benefit themselves, others, and their environment. Ask them to share ways in which they can use their caring strengths to set goals based on what they have learned in their science classes.

Social Studies

The social sciences relate to our study and understanding of people the world over. People establish governments, laws, people-helping-people programs, and institutions in the name of caring. In the social sciences, children can learn about caring for distant others, caring for ideas, and caring for the environment. These are major areas of caring and often represent significant challenges to those who are involved. Help your children explore *ideas* that people have cared and died for since the beginning of time. Help children learn some caring strategies that will help people to solve their differences peacefully (negotiation, mediation, conflict resolution, peacemaking, and peacekeeping). Examine caring strengths that children can learn that will help them to live in harmony with people who are different from them. Cooperation, kindness, caring, respect, compassion, self-discipline, giving, perseverance, and honesty are virtues needed in building caring communities. Help your children appreciate and experience diversity as a strength. Explore various local, regional, national, and global programs of a caring nature that people support in helping to improve the quality of life for all human beings. Help your children see ways in which they can participate in the building of a caring global community.

Health and Physical Education

Perhaps the one subject area in which children are most familiar when it comes to caring is health and physical education. Everything that children learn results in the development of caring strengths that they can use to benefit themselves and others. Help children understand that they are responsible for their own health and safety. Explore with them caring choices they can make when it comes to exercise, nutrition, rest, participation in sports, recreational activities (swimming, boating, bicycling, skateboarding, walking, hiking), and doing things at home (mowing, climbing ladders, using chemicals). Help your children explore caring choices in the seven centers of care and how these choices impact the health and wellness of all people.

TIPS FOR CAREGIVERS

Continue to emphasize that life has value. You and your children are now ready to explore and participate in the seven centers of care. You will be helping your children understand the nature of caring, which is to show concern and to demonstrate interest on behalf of oneself, others, and the environment. The ideas, suggestions, and activities that follow will expose you and your children to the seven centers of care and the vast number of caring experiences that await those who care.

Caring for Self

1. Help your children to develop their own health and wellness maintenance log. This plan can be fashioned to replicate a vehicular maintenance-plan checklist. Provide space in this plan to record the dates of regular vision, hearing, dental, and physical exams. Provide space to record needed immunizations and medications that need to be taken. The rest of the health and wellness log should be devoted to such topics as nutrition, daily physical exercise, grooming, and hygiene. You and your children can decide upon a list of caring activities for each of these topics. As children participate in each of these daily activities, they check them off to demonstrate their completion. If guidance is needed in developing this log, ask your physician or school nurse.

2. Brainstorm a list of self-care activities that children can practice. Here are a few ideas:
   - Listen to relaxing music
   - Take slow, deep breaths
   - Imagine pleasant thoughts
   - Picture relaxing scenes
   - Read a fun book
   - Take a long walk.

3. Select ideas from the above list and use them to care for yourself daily.

Caring for Family and Friends

1. Brainstorm with your children a list of caring ideas they can practice when caring for family and friends. Here are a few ideas. As you think of more things to do, add them to this list:
   - Write thank-you notes to people who have cared for you
   - Give hugs and kisses
   - Give compliments
   - Demonstrate respect (listen to others, respect privacy, address others in kind and caring ways)
   - Share ideas, concerns, hurts, and feelings
   - Offer praise and words of encouragement
   - Provide assistance to those in need
   - Follow the Golden Rule
   - Use caring words
   - Practice caring deeds
   - Take turns
   - Use good manners
   - Treat others fairly
   - Resolve conflict peacefully
   - Cooperate with and encourage others
   - Accept responsibility for your actions
   - Use your sense of humor in caring ways.
2. Continue to add ideas and suggestions to the above list. Place all of these ideas in a jar. Pull ideas daily from the caring jar and use them to care for family members and friends.

Caring for Acquaintances and Distant Other

Caring for those we do not know well, or at all, is important in helping to build caring communities. Here are a few ideas to consider:

1. Brainstorm a list of the different places you go or visit where you have contact with people you don't know well or have never met. Some examples might be:
   - Doctor's office
   - Shopping malls
   - Supermarkets

- Restaurants
- Parks and recreation sites
- Movie theaters.

2. Now brainstorm a list of caring choices that you can make in the presence of people at these sites. Some ideas to consider are the following:
   - Opening and closing doors for people
   - Saying "thank you," "please," and "may I"
   - Giving directions
   - Asking questions politely
   - Smiling
   - Offering help to others in need
   - Writing letters and cards to people in hospitals and nursing homes
   - Thanking people locally and nationally for their acts of caring
   - Treating others with respect
   - Participating in community service projects.

Caring for Nonhuman Animals

1. Involve your children in caring activities that improve the quality of life for pets, domestic animals, and animals of the wild. Brainstorm a list of caring activities in which your children can participate. Here are a few suggestions:
   - Visit your local animal shelter and learn ways that you can become involved; volunteer your services
   - Adopt an endangered animal and learn what you can do to care for it
   - Feed, water, shelter, and provide assistance to animals and birds in need of care
   - Have your children brainstorm a list of things they can do to care for their pets (water, feed, exercise, shelter) and then assist them in providing that care.

Caring for Plants and the Environment

1. Help your children to understand the many ways in which plants care for them. Plants provide people with food, medicines, clothing,

oxygen, filter air, prevent soil erosion; they provide shelter and protection to animals and fish; and they provide people with jobs (farmers, lumber jacks, plant shop owners, conservationists, landscapers, and so on).

2. Involve your children in the care of plants at home, in school, and in their communities. Brainstorm the kind of care that plants need and then involve your children in providing that care. Plants need food, water, sunshine, good soil, ground cover to hold moisture, and so on.

3. Explore with your children how their environment cares for them through clean air, land, and water. Ask your children to name different ways that people enjoy the land, air, and water. Ask them to consider what life would be like if they could no longer swim, fish, boat, hunt, hike, camp, walk in the woods, or watch animals and birds in the wild.

4. Have your children brainstorm a list of things they can do to care for the land, air, and water. Invite them to ask other people to offer additional suggestions that they can add to their list. Involve your children in projects, large and small, in caring for their environment.

Caring for the Human-Made World of Objects and Instruments

1. Children live in a world of objects and instruments that help them to care for themselves, others, and the environment. Help them identify objects and instruments at home, in school, and in their communities and what they are designed to do.

2. Explore with your children the importance of caring for objects and instruments so that they will take care of them. Identify objects and instruments and the care they require (bicycles, smoke detectors, lawn mowers, computers, books, and so on).

3. Ask children to consider what life would be like if they did not have toys, computers, television, medical instruments, automobiles, airplanes, houses, lights, and so on. The list is endless, and so is the care objects and instruments provide in improving the quality of life in all seven centers of care.

Caring for Ideas

1. Help your children to understand that ideas provide direction in life. Ideas help people care for themselves and care in the remaining centers of care. Ideas appear in song titles and lyrics, documents (the Constitution, Bill of Rights, Gettysburg Address), sayings, and in literature. Help your children to identify caring ideas to live by:
   - The Golden Rule
   - The Ten Commandments
   - Daily exercise
   - Always telling the truth
   - Ideas governing proper etiquette
   - Good manners
   - Wearing a seat belt when riding in a motor vehicle
   - Being kind to others
   - Considering honesty the best policy
   - Treating others fairly.
2. Help your children identify caring ideas about which people feel strongly. Help your children understand that caring ideas are cared for by practicing them. Help them explore caring ideas that they practice daily.
3. Ask your children to explore caring ideas about which they feel strongly. Help them to explore caring ideas that they practice daily.

3

HELPFUL HABITS—HURTFUL HABITS

DEFINITION

Habit: Something that is done on a regular basis the repetition of which is highly predictable. These automatic patterns of action (Thinking, Feeling, and Acting) can facilitate or inhibit caring and being careful in the seven centers of care.

BACKGROUND INFORMATION

Habits—are they helpful or hurtful? How can one tell the difference between helpful and hurtful habits? Is it possible to learn new habits and eliminate unwanted habits or eliminate habits altogether? What would life be like in the absence of habits? These are but a few of the many questions that we will explore as we consider the benefits and pitfalls of habits in relationship to caring and being careful in the seven centers of care.

Habits are learned behaviors that are practiced repeatedly and consistently in response to specific environmental conditions until they become patterns of action that are automatic and difficult to break. Habits of the body include such behaviors as brushing teeth after meals; putting on a seat belt after entering a motor vehicle; looking to the left, right, and left again before crossing the street; smoking tobacco products; drinking alcohol; using inappropriate language; and teasing others. Habits of the mind include practicing pleasant thoughts, being hopeful and optimistic, using self-affirmations, thinking irrationally, and jumping to conclusions.

Habits practiced by families, ethnic communities, and groups of people sharing similar backgrounds are referred to as *customs*. Customs are often passed from generation to generation; they can be religious, cultural and racial, marital, or of other kinds.

Traditions are habits that exist in families, communities, and cultures. They are established actions or patterns of behavior practiced over time. The ways in which birthdays are celebrated, the types of clothing worn at special events, the manners in which specific holidays are experienced, and ways that various ceremonial practices are conducted often relate to long-standing traditions with particular historical and present-day significance.

Habits that represent a patterned sequence of actions and are practiced daily are often referred to as *routines*. Teachers establish classroom routines, parents practice child-rearing routines, and groups of people establish routines that become *norms* that shape the actions of group members.

Benefits of Habits

Habits, practiced over time, become quite comfortable and help shape the people that we become. Aristotle once said that the habits formed in childhood make no small difference—rather, they make all the difference. When a particular habit becomes established, whether helpful or hurtful to self, others, or the environment, its impact will be felt for a lifetime.

In addition to feeling comfortable and shaping lives, habits have many protective factors in that they help children and adults to:

- Decrease their reaction time in performing routine behaviors
- Preserve their energy
- Perform routine behaviors with consistency and predictability.

Decrease Reaction Time

Fast reaction time is a by-product of consistent and repetitive practice. With practice, routines like the following can be executed safely, quickly, and with accuracy:

- Dialing 911 in emergency situations
- Exiting buildings quickly in response to fire alarms
- Handling emergency situations at home or school (choking, physical injury, natural disasters, and so on)
- Executing sports plays
- Following the same path of travel to and from school.

Once learned, routines like these can be practiced quickly, because they require little or no thought to execute. Explore with your children some of the habits that people in various professions learn so they can lower their reaction time while managing safe and predictable outcomes in the service of others.

Preserve Energy

Habits can bring order, safety, security, and routine into children's lives. Habits connect children to themselves, others, and their environment and allow them to perform daily routines in the absence of thought. Because thinking requires time and energy, habits become time and energy savers in those areas of children's lives where the same routines are performed frequently, if not daily. Children are encouraged to develop habits in areas like the following and use the time and energy saved for life situations that require thought and decision making:

- Brushing their teeth after meals
- Wearing seat belts in motor vehicles
- Keeping a clean room (bed making, clothes hanging, etc.)
- Doing daily chores
- Saying "thank you," "please," and "may I"
- Giving compliments
- Practicing self-affirmations
- Feeding pets.

The list of energy-saving habits is endless. Many additional caring habits can be identified in each of the seven centers of care and added to the list.

Perform Behaviors with Consistency and Predictability

In addition to decreasing reaction time and saving energy, habits produce consistent and predictable results, because they are practiced the same way under similar conditions. The primary reasons for desiring consistent and predictable results are safety and success. While nothing we do is completely safe, caring habits can go a long way in reducing the amount of danger (harm) to which children and adults are subjected.

In addition to safety, caring habits also tend to increase the attainment of desired outcomes (success). Caring and helpful habits thus help ensure, with a high degree of predictability, that children will attain success through their actions. Safety and success are two good reasons for children to learn and practice caring and helpful habits in the seven centers of care. Some examples of caring habits that yield safety and success with uncommon predictability are:

- Using good study habits
- Establishing a daily homework completion routine
- Listening to others
- Treating others with respect
- Smiling
- Treating oneself and others with kindness
- Practicing good grooming daily.

Habits that increase safety and success are worthy of our attention. Helping children develop such habits is necessary if children are to become responsible givers and receivers of care.

Helpful and Hurtful Habits

Habits serve a very real and useful purpose in children's lives. However, habits need to be evaluated in terms of their potential to help or to hurt. Helpful habits need to be encouraged, taught, and maintained, while those that have the potential to do harm must be discouraged and eliminated.

Helpful Habits

Helping children to tell the difference between helpful and hurtful habits is our challenge. I believe that two methods can be used to do this. First, helpful habits have some redeeming qualities to them. They are based on Right, Reality, and Responsibility. They are considered to be *right* things to do. Right habits are legal in that they violate no laws. They are ethical in that they meet societal standards of appropriate human conduct, and they are moral in that they meet acceptable standards of basic goodness. They are habits that will be helpful to self, others, and the environment.

In addition to being a Right thing to do, helpful habits must pass the Reality test. Reality speaks to the evidence that exists in support of a habit. For example, it is a known fact that "stop, drop, and roll" is a helpful action to take in caring for oneself in a burning building. The reality is that "stop, drop, and roll" is the right thing to do in caring and being careful when exposed to fire. Helpful habits are also Responsible habits. Responsible habits receive the approval of parents, teachers, law enforcement personnel, and religious leaders. They are habits that are judged to be positive, caring, and safe, and they result in caring outcomes that improve the quality of life for those who practice them and who are touched by their impact.

A second method for judging the helpfulness of a habit is to examine the environment in which the habit is to be practiced. If the environment remains relatively stable, the habit will produce predictable results. For example, fires in buildings burn in a rather predictable manner. Therefore "stop, drop, and roll" becomes a useful habit in reducing one's risk to serious injury. However, environments that are constantly changing make habits dangerous, in that the results of a static response executed in a fluid situation are totally unpredictable. For example, children who get into the habit of opening the door to their homes in response to a knock may be placing themselves in danger, because they can never predict who may be on the other side of the door.

Helpful habits are thus based on Right, Reality, and Responsibility and are practiced under similar environmental conditions. The following habits are generally considered helpful habits in that they pass both tests previously discussed:

- Smiling
- Using manners
- Brushing teeth daily
- Listening to others
- Crossing at crosswalks
- Taking turns.

However, a word of caution is necessary! Even the habits listed here can have negative consequences if they are practiced under environmental conditions that do not warrant their use, like smiling at someone who has just suffered a serious injury.

Hurtful Habits

Hurtful habits are just as easily learned as helpful habits. However, hurtful habits place children and others at risk of being harmed and therefore need to be stopped before harm can take its toll. Hurtful habits are usually acquired through practice rather than being specifically identified and deliberately taught to children. However, hurtful habits possess some of the same qualities as helpful habits. These qualities, beneficial to helpful habits, place children at risk when hurtful habits are practiced. The qualities of which I speak are the following:

- Habits are automatic and are executed in the absence of thought
- Habits are executed with speed
- Habits are practiced with consistency
- Habits produce highly reliable and predictable outcomes.

Hurtful habits place children in unprotected and vulnerable positions. These habits are not likely to disappear on their own, in that they are ingrained and conditioned to emerge when triggered by the right environmental conditions or thoughts. They are often difficult to break, and yet the price of not trying to diminish their occurrence is too high to pay. Some examples of hurtful habits that children are developing at an alarmingly high rate are:

- Using tobacco products and alcohol
- Developing unhealthy eating habits

- Watching television for several hours a day
- Exhibiting violent behaviors in response to conflict
- Developing a sedentary lifestyle
- Teasing and bullying

These hurtful habits and others like them are being practiced at home, in schools, on playgrounds, and in society. They go against the very nature of caring, cooperation, inclusion, and community building. Damage that hurtful habits inflict is costly for children and society; by working together, we can help children to benefit from habits and not be hurt by them.

Habits and the Seven Centers of Care

Within each of the seven centers of care are habits that children display. Some of these habits are helpful and caring, while others are harmful and potentially dangerous. The goal of habit formation is for children to learn and practice habits of a helpful and caring nature. These habits begin as well thought out behaviors that meet the criteria for helpful and caring habits.

We want children to develop helpful habits in the seven centers of care and to recognize and stop those that place themselves, others, and the environment in harm's way. Some examples of caring habits in each of the centers of care are identified in the paragraphs that follow.

Caring for Self

Children must learn to care for themselves physically, emotionally, intellectually, and spiritually. They must strive to attain optimal health through the life choices they make. Some health care situations require children to think and choose actions with caring and healthful consequences, while other health care strategies become caring habits that are practiced routinely. Some examples of helpful and caring habits are:

Physical Health Habits
- Exercise daily
- Eat a healthy diet

- Practice healthful grooming (skin, hair, nails, feet, wear clean cloth-ing, etc.)
- Obtain adequate sleep (seven to eight hours daily)
- Go for regular checkups (eyes, ears, teeth, body)
- Engage in injury-prevention and safety practices.

Emotional Health Habits
- Express feelings in responsible and healthy ways
- Practice daily self-affirmations
- Practice daily stress-reduction exercises
- Visualize the positive side of life and living.

Intellectual Health Habits
- Practice helpful study habits
- Take daily breaks to energize
- Practice rational thinking
- Set realistic goals (time management)
- Focus on one thing at a time.

Spiritual Health Habits

Spiritual health is about helping children to view themselves as caring human beings whose life purpose it is to make caring choices in the seven centers of care. We want children to practice the habit of asking them-selves four life-defining questions in relation to the life choices they make:

1. Are my life choices helping me to *be* a caring person?
2. What am I *doing* to be a caring person?
3. What caring attributes do I *have* that make me a caring person?
4. Am I *giving* to myself, others, and the environment the best car-ing me I can be?

Caring for Intimate Others, Acquaintances, and Distant Others

Children need to practice caring habits in relation to family and friends and with people about whom they know little (acquaintances and distant others). Because life has value, it is worthy of their care. It takes a community of caregivers and receivers of care to build cooperation, inclusion, and community, such that people belong and are appreciated for who they are and for what they can become. Some caring habits that children can practice are the following:

- Smiling
- Listening to others
- Taking turns
- Sharing
- Giving compliments
- Offering assistance to those in need
- Using good manners ("please," "thank you," "may I")
- Treating others fairly
- Following the Golden Rule
- Obeying the rules
- Demonstrating respect for all people
- Practicing perspective-taking.

Encourage your children to add more caring habits to this list and to practice them often in giving and receiving care.

Caring for Nonhuman Animals

Animals (domestic and wild) give much to our quality of life. They are fun to observe with our eyes and our ears. They help to sustain the balance of nature; provide food and clothing; aid in medical research; and offer invaluable service as entertainers, protectors, comforters, and helpers as caring, dutiful, and loyal companions.

While animals give so much, they must likewise receive the care of others if they are to keep on giving. Some caring habits that children are encourage to learn and practice are the following:

- Approach all animals with care
- Exercise animals daily
- Feed and water animals daily
- Provide clean and sanitary living conditions
- Provide regular medical care
- Follow all hunting and fishing rules

- Observe all animal-protection guidelines
- Become involved in animal-rights-protection activities.

Caring for Plants and the Environment

As with animals and pets, our plant life and physical environment (regional and global) cannot care for us unless caring habits are practiced by all people. Caring habits are needed to sustain healthy vegetation and clean air, land, and water. Many people believe that whatever ails humankind, the answer to health and wellness is to be found in the environment. This statement will hold true if we do not inadvertently destroy a part of ourselves by careless habits that make it impossible to reclaim or restore the environment.

We can and must help children develop caring environmental health habits that will in turn help them sustain the balance of nature and their good health. Some helpful habits to consider include having children:

- Water and feed plant life
- Recycle trash and environmental waste
- Follow rules designed to protect the environment
- Learn ways to protect our natural resources
- Practice personal safety when caring for plants and the environment
- Protect national and state parks from misuse and abuse.

Encourage children to think of additional habits they can practice in support of a global environment that will foster good health for all.

Caring for the Human-Made World of Objects and Instruments

Children's lives and personal well-being depend on the proper care and use of objects and instruments. We therefore need to help children develop safe and caring habits regarding their use, as well as help them to guard against their misuse and abuse. Children demonstrate their care for objects and instruments when they:

- Read and follow all safety and instructional guidelines regarding their proper storage, maintenance, and use

- Conduct regular safety checks and make repairs in accordance with manufacturer recommendations
- Refrain from using objects and instruments in need of repair
- Discard objects and instruments safely when they are no longer working or are unsafe to use.

Challenge your children to think of additional helpful habits that can be added to this list. Identify specific objects and instruments that children use at home and in school. See how many caring habits they can name and learn for each object identified. For example, what helpful habits can children identify regarding writing instruments (pens and pencils), computer printers, smoke alarms, books, playground equipment, and so on?

Caring for Ideas

Children depend on many life lessons (caring ideas) that help them to care for themselves, others, and the environment. These ideas come in the form of sayings, song titles, musical lyrics, poems, words of wisdom, proverbs, laws, rules, guidelines, and commandments.

Caring ideas provide children with an internal guidance system that helps them to distinguish right from wrong with respect to their actions. Caring ideas become habits when they are practiced routinely and guide children in their daily living. Some caring ideas worthy of repetition are found in the following:

- The Golden Rule
- The Ten Commandments
- The Preamble to the Constitution
- The Bill of Rights
- Proper etiquette
- Good manners
- Healthy living guidelines (strategies for self-care)
- Safety rules and regulations
- Environmental protection guidelines.

Once again, this is only a partial list of caring-idea habits. Ask children to identify sayings, song titles, poems, and lyrics that contain words to live by and discuss their meaning. Have them share some of their caring behaviors and the caring ideas (habits) that support them:

- Telling the truth
- Being kind to others
- Wearing their seat belt
- Saying "thank you," "please," and "may I."

Habit Breaking and Habit Making

Habits are learned behaviors that are practiced frequently, if not daily, in the absence of thought. They are, by the same tokens, often difficult to stop. The good news is that with patience, persistence, and a plan, harmful habits can be curtailed and helpful habits developed. For example, many children have stopped unwanted habits—such as nail biting, hitting, name calling, negative self-talk, and talking out in class—and they have learned helpful habits like exercising daily, eating healthy foods, and using good manners.

Children will want to give themselves ample time (patience) to develop a new habit or break an unwanted habit. They will need to motivate themselves to stick with what they are doing until they experience success (persistence). They will also need a plan to follow that will guide them in a positive direction. Lastly, they will need to practice the plan until the hurtful habit is broken or the helpful habit is learned.

The plan is a critical component of habit making and habit breaking. The plan that follows consists of four steps that when followed will bring desired results in developing helpful habits or in stopping hurtful habits.

Step 1: Take Inventory

Whether stopping a hurtful habit or learning a helpful habit, children first need to take inventory of their personal living habits in the seven centers of care. After taking note of the helpful and hurtful habits they practice in each caring center, they can decide what new helpful habits they would like to learn and which hurtful habits they would like to stop.

Step 2: Select a Habit to Stop/Start

From the list of habits identified in Step 1, children are to select a habit they would like to stop or start.

Step 3: Create a Positive Attitude

Commitment to change begins with a positive attitude. Children need to experience a sense of confidence and encouragement that they will achieve their goals. A positive attitude is more likely to be sustained when children have the caring support of others and a carefully designed plan they can follow (steps to success).

Step 4: Steps to Success

When creating an action plan, it is helpful to review your habit (benefits and pitfalls), create a specific and achievable goal, develop steps to achieve the goal, and evaluate your progress.

Review Your Habit. Help children to understand the new habit to be learned. Describe the behaviors to be learned, the benefits of learning the new habit, and the pitfalls to those who do not practice it. When children are breaking a habit, help them understand the habit to be stopped, the harm that comes from practicing it, and the benefits to be experienced when the habit is stopped.

Create a Specific and Achievable Goal. Clear, realistic, and achievable goals are necessary conditions of success. A helpful goal statement contains the *why, what, when, where, who,* and *how* components that will help children to create a specific and achievable goal: *Why* do I want to do this? *What* do I want? *When* will I begin? *Where* will I work on this goal? *Who* will help me? *How* will I achieve my goal (steps), and *how* will I know when I have succeeded?

Develop Steps. What steps will be taken in either stopping a hurtful habit or developing a helpful habit? Steps can be generated from information obtained from people with experience regarding this habit, printed information, and from brainstorming possible steps that can be taken. Evaluate each step and then sequence them. Children will need assistance from caring adults in creating the steps to success.

Evaluate Your Progress. Encourage children to evaluate their progress toward goal attainment. If the goal is stated clearly and the steps to be followed are specific and achievable, children will be able to determine if what they are doing is working. Continued practice will result in habit formation.

Modification in this process can be made to accommodate both the facilitator's teaching methods and the child's learning style. These four general steps have been incorporated into an easy-to-follow, four-part Habit Training Action Plan that children can use in helping them to develop a helpful habit or to stop a hurtful one. The Habit Training Action Plan is found in the activities section of this chapter.

ROLE OF THE FACILITATOR

Developing helpful habits and stopping hurtful habits in the seven centers of care constitute the focus of chapter 3. Learning to care and be careful begins with developing and maintaining helpful caring habits that will last a lifetime. As facilitator, your role is to help children understand the value of possessing and practicing helpful caring habits. You will be helping them understand the role that habits play in their lives and explore the many caring and helpful habits found in the centers of care. You will be helping them to explore their own habits and how they impact their lives and life around them.

Encourage your children to look at all the habits they practice from the time they get up in the morning until they go to bed at night. They will be surprised at how many they have developed. Help them relate their habit list to the seven centers of care and classify their habits as being helpful, hurtful, and "not sure." Help them understand that there is always room for self-improvement in this area of their lives. Anything they do to self-improve increases their value and the positive impact they can have in helping themselves and others care and be careful.

Once your children understand the value of habits and the role that habits play in caring and being careful, you will be able to help them to:

- Stop unhealthy, unsafe, careless, and hurtful habits
- Choose healthy, safe, caring, and helpful habits to learn

- Commit to learning these new helpful habits
- Practice these helpful behaviors until they become helpful habits
- Identify opportunities in the seven centers of care to practice their new habits.

Have fun helping your children to understand and value the importance that habits play in caring and being careful. This chapter contains many interesting and thought-provoking activities, as well as a Habit Training Action Plan that will help you to help your children become "creatures of helpful habits" based on Right, Reality, and Responsibility (Three Rs).

BENEFITS TO CHILDREN

Children who learn caring and helpful habits:

- Practice helpful habits based on the Three Rs
- Act quickly and responsibly in response to life situations that threaten their safety
- Have more time and energy to spend on life situations requiring problem solving and decision making
- Achieve success on the basis of consistent and predictable responses.

PITFALLS TO CHILDREN

Children who do not learn helpful habits:

- Place themselves, others, and the environment in danger
- Display slower reaction times and inconsistent responses to life situations that threaten their safety
- Spend more time and energy on deciding what to do in response to repetitious and routine situations
- Produce inconsistent and unreliable responses in repetitious and routine situations.

ACTIVITIES

Creatures of Habit

Objectives

1. To help children understand the meaning of habit
2. To help children recognize that they are "creatures of habit"
3. To help children name some of their habits.

Group Size: Classroom group
Time Required: 30 minutes
Materials: Chalkboard and chalk
Facilitator: Help your children to recognize that habits represent routine, automatic patterns of thought and behaviors that are practiced without thinking. Because habits are automatic and practiced routinely in the absence of thought, they are often difficult to stop. They are hard to give up also because they become very comfortable. Before you introduce the topic of *habits* to your children, take them through the exercises listed below. Each experience is designed to illustrate the many habits that your children have already developed. Following these activities, you will engage your children in a discussion about habits and relate what they have been experiencing to your discussion. At the conclusion of "Creatures of Habit," your children will understand the meaning of habit and will be able to identify some of their own habits.

Process

Explain to your children that they are going to participate in some exercises that will be followed by a discussion regarding what they have been doing.

Exercise 1: Tell your children to fold their arms over their chest. Have them repeat this behavior but now ask them to reverse the fold. Ask them which fold feels more comfortable and why.

Exercise 2: Tell your children to raise their hand as though they were being called on to answer in class. Now tell them to lower their hand and raise the opposite hand. Ask them which raised hand feels more comfortable and why.

Exercise 3: Tell your children to stand up beside their desks, take three steps forward, and stop. Have them repeat the same exercise again. Ask them to notice which foot (left or right) was used to take the first step. Tell them to repeat the exercise and take the first step with the opposite foot. Ask them which walking exercise felt more comfortable and why.

Discussion

1. Ask your children, now that they have folded their arms, raised their hands, and have taken three steps forward, if they noticed anything about their behaviors each time they repeated the exercises. They will notice that the first performance of each exercise felt more comfortable than the second.
2. Introduce the term *habit* and ask your children if they know what a *habit* is and how it might relate to the exercises that they just performed. Answer: A *habit* is a behavior that you become use to performing repeatedly without thinking and that feels comfortable.
3. Have your children brainstorm some of their habits and list them on the board. If your children are having a difficult time identifying habits, use headings like the following to help them get started:
   a. Health habits (washing hands)
   b. Bicycle safety habits (wearing a helmet)
   c. Pedestrian safety habits (walking facing traffic)
   d. School safety habits (take turns)
   e. Emergency response habits ("stop, drop, and roll")
   f. Environmental protection habits (place papers in trash can)
   g. Safe riding (car) habits (wear seat belts)
   h. Home safety habits (test smoke alarm monthly)
   i. Eating (dinner table) habits (chew with mouth closed)
   j. Good manners habits ("thank you," "please," "may I").

Homework

1. Have your children interview their parents (caregivers), relatives, and friends regarding their habits.
2. Have your children keep a log of their own behaviors. Ask them to identify those behaviors which they think are habits.

3. Be sure to have them consider habits of the mind in their discussion. Habits of the mind are repetitious thought patterns. Some examples of these thoughts are the following perfectionist thoughts:

- I can't make a mistake
- I must be perfect
- You must be perfect to be my friend.

The following irrational thoughts are also habits of mind:

- Nobody likes me; therefore I am unlikable
- Self–name calling
- Put-downs of oneself.

Now, here are some rational positive thoughts:

- I can do it
- I am not perfect, but I can self-improve
- Perform daily self affirmations (mental pats on the back).

Helpful Habits—Hurtful Habits

Objectives

1. To help children recognize that some habits are helpful (safe and caring) while others are hurtful (unsafe and harmful)
2. To help children identify some of their helpful and hurtful habits.

Group Size: Classroom group
Time Required: 15 to 20 minutes
Materials : Index cards (you will need to prepare index cards before participating in the two (2) activities that follow).
Facilitator: Help your children recognize that habits can be beneficial. They can help them to stay safe, decrease their response time, and save time and energy. Habits, like wearing a bicycle safety helmet when riding a bike and walking on the left side of a roadway facing traffic, help to ensure safety. Fire-drill practice and emergency-response dialing of 911 are examples of habits that protect

children by lowering their reaction time in case of danger. Other habits, like brushing teeth, laying out clothes to wear for the next day, exercising, and following study routines, help to save time and energy, because making these helpful tasks automatic allows children to complete them without having to spend time making decisions about them each time.

You will be helping your children to recognize that some habits increase their safety, are caring, and are helpful. You will also be helping them to recognize that habits as a group have a downside as well. While most habits help children to save time and energy and to respond quickly, they may also place them at risk when confronted with dangerous situations. Children who get into the habit of riding in motor vehicles without buckling up or of participating in sports without wearing protective gear increase their risk of injury and even death. The activities that follow will help your children recognize the difference between helpful and hurtful habits and to identify habits of their own that fall into each category.

Process

Activity 1: Helpful Habit Card Game

1. Obtain a pack of three-by-five index cards. On each card write an activity, experience, or life event in which children participate (seven centers of care). For example, you might have cards that read: riding in a car, playing baseball, bicycling, taking care of my family, walking on a roadway, or getting ready for school.
2. For each card that you read to your children, ask them to identify a safe, caring, and helpful habit they could practice. Ask them to indicate how they and others can benefit from practicing this habit.
3. Once your children understand the index-card game, divide your class into groups of three and give each group three cards. Let each child present a card to the group and the remaining two share safe, caring, and helpful habits that could be associated with that card. Invite them to share, with their group, how these habits are beneficial to self, others, or property.

Activity 2: Habits That Hurt/Harm

Some habits are unsafe and hurtful. Ask your children to brainstorm a list of hurtful habits (behaviors) that children their age sometimes practice. For every habit listed, ask them to identify a potential harm that could occur:

- Not brushing teeth—cavities and loss of teeth
- Bullying—loss of friends
- Skateboarding unprotected—injury
- Riding in a car not wearing a seat belt—injury or death.

Teach your children how to discriminate between *helpful* habits and *hurtful* habits using three decision-making filters (Right, Reality, and Responsibility) and the questions that accompany each filter. Following are the questions for Right:

1. Is this a *Right* thing to do? (Yes or no)
2. How will it effect me, others, and property? (Help or hurt).

The following are Reality questions:

1. How do I know this is a right thing to do?
2. Do I have evidence (facts) that this a caring and safe thing to do? (Yes or no).

The following are questions for Responsibility:

1. Do my parents, teachers, and people who love me think this is a safe (right) thing to do? (Yes or no)
2. Will doing this result in a safe and caring outcome for me, others, and the environment? (Yes or no).

For a habit to be *helpful*, it must pass through the three filters. Children must answer yes to all questions, believe that the habit is helpful, and have evidence/facts to support its caring nature.

Now list the following habits on separate index cards and have your children decide, using Right, Reality, and Responsibility, which habits are helpful and which are hurtful. Have them discuss each habit with respect to all three filters before deciding how that habit should be labeled. Place the helpful-habit cards in one pile and the hurtful-habit cards in another. (Young children can participate in this activity by deciding if the habit is helpful or hurtful to themselves, others, or property; for each habit drawn, ask young children to name either a helpful or hurtful outcome.) Here is a list of index-card habits:

- Smoking tobacco products
- Checking bicycle brakes
- Eating a balanced diet
- Setting an alarm at night to get up for school
- Doing homework at the same time each evening
- Petting animals one doesn't know
- Saying "thank you," "please," "may I"
- Walking on the right side of the road
- Sharing my feelings with others
- Boating without a life jacket
- Smiling
- Storing gasoline in the basement
- Walking around lowered railroad track crossing barriers
- Wearing eye-protection glasses when mowing grass
- Checking smoke and carbon monoxide alarms weekly/monthly
- Following school and classroom rules
- Wearing seat belts (car)
- Reviewing schoolwork prior to submitting it
- Turning off the lights
- Brushing teeth after eating
- Crossing the street when traffic light is green
- Eating fruits and vegetables
- Drinking alcohol
- Picking up stranded motorists
- Locking car doors
- Helping other children with their schoolwork

- Getting angry (losing temper)
- Picking up paper lying alongside the road.

Additional habits can replace habits on this list. Children can be asked to brainstorm habits (helpful and hurtful) that can be used to play this game.

Discussion

1. Ask your children to indicate what makes some habits helpful (caring and safe) and others hurtful (unsafe and harmful).
2. Ask your children to identify some of their helpful habits (seven centers of care)—ones of which they are proud.
3. Have your children share with their class some helpful habits they would like to develop.
4. Ask your children to identify some hurtful habits which they have developed.
5. Have your children share with their classmates one or two hurtful habits they would like to stop doing.

Explain to your children that human beings are capable of self-improvement. They can learn to do better by making changes in their lives. One way that they can do better is develop habits that will help them become caring people who care for themselves, others, and the environment. They also can learn to improve themselves by stopping hurtful habits. Let your children know that soon they will be learning how to develop new caring habits and stop hurtful habits. They will be learning how to self-improve.

Habit Making and Habit Breaking

Objective: To help children develop caring, helpful habits and stop hurtful and potentially dangerous habits.

Group Size: Classroom group

Time Required: 30 minutes

Materials: Habit Training Action Plan

Facilitator: Help your children to understand that habits serve useful purposes in their lives. Habits can increase their safety and reduce their risk to danger, decrease their response time when faced with an emergency, and can help them save time and energy by allowing them to act quickly, safely, and predictably without having to think. All children have developed habits, some of which are helpful and enable them to care and to be careful, while other habits place them in danger because they are not based on Right, Reality, and Responsibility. Explain to them that today they are going to learn how to develop helpful and caring habits and what they can do to stop harmful habits that they have learned.

Process

Explain that you will be teaching a four-part Habit Training Action Plan. This plan can be used to teach helpful habits or to stop hurtful habits. The four parts that children will be learning are information, steps to success, confidence building, and opportunity. The new habit that you and the children will be learning together is exiting the school quickly and safely after hearing the fire alarm—a fire-alarm drill.

Information. Explain to your children that all helpful habits are based on important factual information. Tell them you will be giving them information about fire drills and what they are to do when the fire alarm sounds. Explain to them the benefits of learning how to exit a building quickly and in an orderly way, and the pitfalls of not developing this caring habit. Follow the steps provided:

a. Give children a copy of handout 3.1.
b. Ask children if they know what a fire drill is and why we practice them. Explain that fire-drill practice sessions result in the formation of habits. When they hear the bell, they will be able to react quickly and safely in exiting the building because they have learned a new helpful habit.
c. Help children to write their responses to statements 1 and 2 of the handout before answering item 3.
d. *Benefits*: Brainstorm and discuss with your children the benefits of learning how to get out of a burning building quickly and safely (statement 3).
e. *Pitfalls*: Brainstorm and discuss some of the harmful things that can happen to children if they do not develop this helpful habit (statement 4).

f. Provide children with information about fire drills and what they will be learning (statement 5).

Steps to Success. Your children will need to have specific steps they can follow in exiting the school building. Using the information that you have provided your children about fire drills, assist them in brainstorming steps they can take to quickly and safely leave the school building. List their ideas on the chalkboard (statement 6):

a. Discuss and arrange these steps in proper sequence (statement 7).
b. Model and practice each step with your children.
c. Practice all the steps together in sequence.
d. Evaluate the results. Ask your children to identify any problems they had individually and as a class. Ask them what additional ideas they have for getting out of the building faster while continuing to care and to be careful.
e. Continue to practice exiting the school building quickly while striving to improve safety.

Confidence Building. Confidence building can be a result of providing children with feedback and encouragement letting them know how they are doing. Confidence building motivates and energizes the learning process. Confidence building occurs throughout the four-part process. You build confidence when you model everything that you teach, provide practice time, move at a comfortable pace, allow for mistakes, avoid being punitive, offer praise, and teach children how to give themselves a pat on the back (self-affirmation). Go over the confidence builders that are listed on handout 3.1 (statement 8).

Opportunity. Many behaviors never become habits because children do not apply what they have learned. Take time to explore with children when and how they can practice their fire-drill habit. For example, children can practice it in their minds. This is called *mental rehearsal.* They can discuss with their parents, caregivers, and family members the importance of having and practicing a fire-drill plan at home. Children can also apply their new habit by noticing where the exits are when entering unfamiliar buildings and by formulating a mental plan of escape for use should they need to leave a building safely and quickly. Review statements 9 and 10 with your children and have them respond to these two items.

Discussion

1. Have your children discuss the importance of developing helpful habits and how they and others benefit from their use.
2. Help your children understand that helpful habits first begin as carefully thought out "habit training action plans" based on Right, Reality, and Responsibility. Ask them to discuss whether their fire alarm drill habit meets the Three Rs and why they believe this is the case.
3. Explore with your children various careers that require people to develop helpful habits. Explore helpful habits that firefighters, police officers, medical emergency response teams, and the military practice and use frequently, if not daily.
4. Ask your children to consider some helpful habits they can practice as pedestrians, occupants of vehicles, playground users, and as health-conscious people.
5. Ask your children to identify a new helpful habit they would like to learn. Ask them to develop a plan using the handout 3.1. Encourage them to seek the help of others and use whatever resources they can obtain to develop their action plan. Once completed, encourage your children to follow their plan and learn a new helpful habit.

From "I Can't" to "I Can"

Objectives

1. To help children stop the hurtful habit of negative thinking
2. To help children recycle "I can't" thoughts into "I can" thoughts.

Group Size: Classroom group
Time Required: 30 minutes
Materials: paper, colored markers/crayons, two clean metal vegetable cans per child, two can labels per child

HABIT TRAINING ACTION PLAN

Part 1: Information

1. I want to learn (stop) the following habit: _____

2. Describe the habit you want to learn/stop: _____

3. How will I and others benefit (be helped) from learning (stopping) this habit? _____

_____

4. What pitfalls (hurtful outcomes) are likely to occur if I don't learn (stop) this habit? _____

_____

5. What information do I need to have that will help me to learn (stop) this habit? Where can I get this information, and who can help me get it? _____

_____

_____

Part 2: Steps to Success

6. Brainstorm steps that you can take to learn (stop) this habit: _____

_____

7. List the steps in the order they will be practiced and begin:

   a. _____

   b. _____

   c. _____

   e. _____

   f. _____

(continued on next page)

Handout 3.1

HABIT TRAINING ACTION PLAN *(continued)*

Part 3: Confidence

8. Make sure you do not become discouraged. If you feel like giving up, do the following:

   - Ask your teacher or a family member for help.
   - Take small steps in learning (stopping) your habit.
   - Allow yourself to make mistakes. That is how you learn.
   - Practice your habit a little at a time giving yourself time to rest.
   - Give yourself a pat on the back and words of encouragement.
   - Practice positive thinking.
   - Other ideas

Part 4: Opportunity

9. Make a list of the times and places where you can *start* using this new habit (stop using a hurtful habit): _____

_____

10. Write your list (opportunities to practice) on a 3 × 5 index card and carry it with you as a reminder to practice your habit (stop using a hurtful habit).

Note: Some children may find it helpful to create and follow a contract. Behavior contracts can be motivators and reminders of what children have committed themselves to doing. Contracts usually include the child's name, what the child plans to do (steps to be taken), the first step to be taken, a starting date, a completion date, places for signatures (child and witness) and signing dates.

Handout 3.1

Facilitator: Most children engage in some negative thinking about themselves. Negative thinking, practiced over time, becomes habitual and damaging. Negative thinking depletes children's positive energy, reduces motivation, lowers their self-esteem, and diminishes their love and respect of themselves. You can help children to challenge their "I can't" thinking and to recycle their thoughts into more positive and realistic statements.

Process

1. Ask children to review the definition of a habit.
2. Ask your children if they have ever caught themselves saying "I can't."
3. Explore some of these statements with your children. For example: "I can't draw." "I can't sing." I can't do math." "I can't (fill in the blank)."
4. Ask your children if they know what it means to recycle. Explain to them that their parents or family members may take old newspapers, cans, glass, and cardboard to a recycling center, which collects it and later takes it to companies that make these "unwanted" materials into new and useful products.
5. Explain to your children that you and they are going to practice recycling "I can't" statements into "I can" statements.
6. Give each child two empty aluminum cans and two clean labels (slips of paper to go around each can). Have them write "I can't" on one label and " I can" on the other. After decorating their labels, they are to place them on the two cans. Each child now has an "I can" can and an "I can't" can.
7. Discuss with your children the meaning of "I can't." Ask them how it feels when they say "I can't [fill in the blank]." Explain to your children that when they say "I can't" to themselves it stops them from trying. They feel powerless and discouraged.
8. Explain to your children that "I can't" means that they believe that they are incapable of performing a specific task. Tell your children that in most cases it isn't that they can't do something, just that they don't know how.

9. Now ask your children what it feels like when they say "I can" and really believe that they can do what they set out to do. Help your children to understand that "I can" statements feel good, help them to feel powerful, and provide them with the encouragement to try.

10. I *can'ts* can be recycled into I *cans* by obtaining answers to the following questions: Who can help me? What can I read? What is the first step I can take?

11. Now teach your children how they can recycle the statement, "I can't draw," by following three steps to success:

    a. It's not that I *can't* draw. I *don't know how* to draw. Who can help me? What can I read?

    b. I *can* learn how to draw.

    c. The first step I can take is (fill in the blank).

11. Help your children to list some of their "I can't" statements.

12. Now have them select one of their "I can't" statements and turn it into an "I can" statement using the three steps presented earlier.

13. Challenge your children to recycle their "I can'ts" into "I cans" by recognizing that with patience, persistence, and a plan (three steps to success) they can become "I can" people.

Discussion

1. Ask your children to discuss how saying "I can't" is a hurtful habit to practice and what steps they can take to break the habit.

2. Ask your children to read and discuss Edgar Guest's poem "It Couldn't Be Done."

3. Explore with your children the names of people and things they accomplished when others were telling them, "It can't be done." People like the Wright brothers, Thomas Edison, Robert Fulton, Abraham Lincoln, and Henry Ford were told that what they were trying to do could not be done, but they persevered and did it. With patience, persistence, and a plan they overcame many life obstacles on their way to achieving success. They beat the odds, and so can you.

SUGGESTED ACTIVITIES FOR THE WEEK

Language Arts and Reading

Have your children identify helpful habits they can develop when caring for themselves, intimate others, acquaintances and distant others, nonhuman animals, plants and the physical environment, the human-made world of objects and instruments, and ideas. Have children read stories, write papers, and make presentations that identify and highlight the virtues of caring habits in the seven centers of care. As children observe caring habits being practiced by others, they can provide these people with positive feedback in recognition of their kind and caring actions.

Math

Children are encouraged to develop caring habits with respect to reading food labels and using the information to "eat healthy." They are likewise encouraged to take their pulse rate before and after exercise and to monitor their own blood pressure readings in maintaining sound cardiovascular health. Children can also practice the habit of checking their math work, maintaining proper air pressure in their bicycle tires, and counting their change after a purchase.

Science

As you study the various sciences, help your children to see the value of caring habits, habits that save lives, reduce injury, and help people to live healthy and wellness-oriented lifestyles. Habits like the following are critical in the sciences:

- Wearing protective eyewear
- Following directions
- Attending to detail
- Wearing protective clothing
- Following prescribed protocols
- Guarding against contamination.

Have your children explore needed environmental habits that people must practice if our planet is to flourish. Ask your children, when they are studying animal and plant life, to examine habits that can destroy and habits that can enhance and benefit all living things. Explore with your children careless habits that have resulted in injury and loss of life. Help your children to explore scientific and technological advances that require caring habits.

When preparing and storing food and cooking meals, discuss the importance that habits play in helping to ensure their safety. Help your children to understand the value of caring habits and the devastation that can occur when unsafe, hurtful habits are practiced in the seven centers of care.

Social Studies

Caring for self, intimate others, and acquaintances and distant others relate to social studies. Help your children understand that they are social animals. The kind of people they will become is dependent on their behaviors and the behaviors of others. Caring habits that facilitate peace and encourage cooperation, trust, friendship, and group problem-solving are needed if people of diverse backgrounds are to live together. Help your children discover and practice caring habits that bring people together. Habits like smiling, sharing, taking turns, giving positive feedback, listening, and respecting others can be taught and practiced. Many social skills, once learned and practiced, become very effective social habits that can help to maintain peace even during times of heated social debate.

Health and Physical Education

Help your children to identify self-caring habits they can develop that will benefit them. Some examples of self-care habits are: brushing teeth, bathing, combing hair, exercising daily, eating healthy foods, and getting enough rest. In addition, discuss with your children the vast number of safety habits they can develop relating to bicycle safety, home safety, pedestrian safety, sports and summer activity safety, and playground safety. Developing sound, caring safety habits are children's first defense against serious injury and premature death. Take the time to impress upon your children that habits can work for them or against them. They need to be wise in discriminating the safe from the unsafe when it comes to the habits that they learn and practice.

TIPS FOR CAREGIVERS

Habits are automatic patterns of learned behaviors fixed through repetition. They are practiced repeatedly and consistently in the absence of thought. Habits can be very helpful to your children, in that they can be performed quickly and with consistency. Consequently, we teach children, through repetition, how to exit a school building safely and quickly when the fire alarm sounds. We also teach children life-saving measures they can perform if caught in a fire, such as "stop, drop, and roll." These two habits save lives. Other safe and caring habits that you can teach your children to perform are:

- Brushing their teeth after meals
- Practicing good daily hygiene
- Exercising daily
- Reading food labels
- Cooking foods at the proper temperatures
- Wearing seat belts when riding in motor vehicles
- Using good manners.

This is only a partial list of helpful caring habits. You will be learning about other helpful habits and how you can teach them to your children. However, as helpful as habits can be, they can also place your children in harm's way. Some hurtful habits include using tobacco products, eating foods high in sugar and saturated fats, watching hours of television instead of exercising, staying up late and not obtaining enough rest, and jaywalking in heavy traffic. Many more example of hurtful habits can be added to this list. These few examples are provided merely to alert you to the dangers to which your children are exposed.

The good news about habits is that you and your children have a choice. Children can be taught helpful habits and learn to identify those that are hurtful so that they can be stopped. The following suggestions, activities, and tips will help you to teach your children about habits and how they impact their lives. The children will learn about helpful and hurtful habits, how to identify each, and steps they can take to learn helpful habits while rejecting those that place them, others, and the environment (seven centers of care) in danger.

1. Tell your children to fold their arms across their chest. Now ask them to reverse the fold. Ask them which fold feels the most comfortable. They will tell you that the first fold feels best. Now ask them if they know what a habit is. Explain to them that a habit is something they do repeatedly without thinking about it. The manner in which they fold their arms over their chest has become a habit.

2. Help your children to explore some habits or routines that they practice. Some examples might include:
   • Brushing their teeth
   • Going to bed at the same time each night
   • Wearing a seat belt when riding in a motor vehicle
   • Saying "please," "thank you," and "may I"
   • Watching a favorite television program.
   Now ask your children to identify (name) one habit they perform in each of the following areas.
   • Health habits (washing hands before eating)
   • Bicycle safety habits (wear a protective helmet)
   • Pedestrian safety habits (walk facing traffic)
   • School safety habits (take turns)
   • Emergency fire safety habits ("stop, drop, roll")
   • Environmental safety habits (pick up trash)
   • Automobile safety habits (wear seat belt)
   • Home safety habits (test smoke alarms the first day of each month)
     • Dinner table habits (chew with your mouth closed)
     • Good manners (say "thank you").

3. Share with your children some helpful and caring habits that you practice yourself.

4. Explain to your children that some habits are helpful (safe and caring) while others can be hurtful (unsafe and harmful). Brainstorm with your children some helpful and hurtful habits.

Now, teach your children a simple, three-step test that will help them to decide if a habit is helpful or hurtful. Use tooth brushing to help them understand how this three-step model works.

Right: How will this effect me, others, and the environment? (Help or hurt). Is this a right thing to do? (Yes or no)

Reality: Do I have proof that this is a caring and helpful thing to do? (Yes or no)

Responsibility: Will my parents, teachers, or people who love me tell me that this is a caring and helpful thing to do? (Yes or no)

For a habit to be caring and helpful, your children must answer yes to all three questions. Have them discuss each question before saying yes or no. If your children are not sure which to answer, provide them with more information or have them talk to people who can give them accurate information about the habit (fact finding) before answering the question.

5. Now that your children understand how to use this simple, three-step test to decide if a habit is helpful or hurtful, write one hurtful habit on each of four index cards. Process each card separately through the three steps. Ask your children the questions presented in the model. Have them discuss their answers and then decide whether to answer yes or no at each step. One no response is all that is needed to declare the habit hurtful.

6. Repeat the previous activity by writing one helpful habit on four separate index cards. Go through the same three steps and have your children discuss each question before answering yes or no. They should be able to answer yes to all three questions for each of the four habits presented.

7. Your children are now ready to play the index-card game "Helpful or Hurtful—This is the Question." Using 20 index cards, write helpful and hurtful habits on each card so that you now have a mix of helpful and hurtful habits in the deck. Ask your children to select the top card from the deck, turn it over, and read the habit that is written. Using the three-step test, they are to decide if the habit is helpful or hurtful and why. After each card is processed it should be placed in one of three piles—helpful, hurtful, "not sure." Some examples of habits to write on your index cards are the following:

- Smoking tobacco products
- Crossing street at crosswalk
- Swimming alone
- Opening the front door when someone knocks
- Turning off house lights not in use
- Smiling
- Petting every dog that you see.

8. Explore with your children some of their habits and write them on index cards. Now process these habits using the same three-step method they learned.

9. Now that your children understand how to recognize helpful and hurtful habits, help them to identify an example of each in the seven centers of care. Here are a few ideas:
   - Caring for myself: exercise daily (helpful), smoke tobacco products (hurtful), eat a heart-health diet (helpful), and eat foods high in sugar and fat (hurtful)
   - Caring for intimate others (family and friends): give smiles, compliments, hugs, and positive attention (helpful); argue, use put-downs, and ignore others (hurtful)
   - Caring for acquaintances and distant others: use good manners (helpful); engage in name calling, labeling others, and fighting (hurtful)
   - Caring for nonhuman animals: approach pets cautiously (helpful); neglect pets (failure to feed, water, and exercise) (hurtful)
   - Caring for plants and the environment: pick up litter whenever you find it (helpful); failure to read and follow park (state and national) rules (hurtful)
   - Caring for objects and instruments: test smoke alarms the first day of each month (helpful); mow lawn without wearing ear plugs (hurtful)
   - Caring for ideas: follow the Golden Rule (helpful); treat those who are different from your poorly (hurtful).

   (Ideas are thoughts, rules, sayings, and beliefs that guide children's action. Ideas become habits when practiced routinely. Some ideas become helpful habits, while other become hurtful. Help your children to identify ideas worthy of their care as well as ideas that are harmful and dangerous.)

10. Teach your children some steps they can take to learn helpful habits and to stop hurtful habits. Here are a few suggestions for habit making and habit breaking.

Step 1: Decide what habit you want to practice. For example, wear bicycle helmet when riding my bicycle.

Step 2: State how learning this habit will be helpful to me, others, or the environment. For example, if I should fall from my bike and hit my head, the helmet will reduce the severity of my injuries. Wearing a helmet will also please my parents. In some states, wearing a helmet is the law.

Step 3: What pitfalls (harm) might come to me, others, or the environment if I don't learn this habit? The answer is, if I don't wear a helmet when I ride my bicycle, I could get badly injured and the people that love me would be sad.

Step 4: Who can help me learn this habit? Possible answers are friends, parents, a bicycle dealer, or a police officer.

Step 5: Brainstorm some steps I can take to practice this habit—things I need to do. Arrange these things in the order they will be practiced. For example, hang the helmet on my bike handle so I will see it, put the helmet on before getting on my bike, adjust the helmet so that it fits properly, and get on my bike and have a caring and safe ride.

Step 6: Do not give up. If you feel like quitting, talk to people who can help you to stay with your plan. For example, you might feel like giving up because the helmet hurts your head or kids tease you when wearing it. Get help from people you know who can help you to develop a plan to address these concerns.

Step 7: Practice, practice, practice. If you practice the same routine over and over again, you will learn to do it well. You will always remember to practice your new habit. It will feel good and become easier and easier to do.

Have fun teaching your children about the value of helpful habits. Have them explore helpful and caring habits that people in various professions practice. Help them see how helpful and caring habits can help them save time, give them more energy, and protect them from harm.

4

CARING AND DANGER

DEFINITION

Danger: Danger relates to one's personal exposure to harm (physical, emotional, intellectual, and spiritual).

BACKGROUND INFORMATION

Danger is a variable condition that all people live with on a daily basis. It is inescapable, for nothing in life is completely safe. Children and adults increase their exposure to danger when they do not make caring choices in the seven centers of care that are based on Right, Reality, and Responsibility.

"What children care for will care for them" is an adage that holds true when caring is based on the Three Rs, but even then, caring is not without danger. The goal of this chapter is not to create fear and inaction but to educate children about the nature of caring and the potential dangers that exist when they care. This knowledge will help children to understand that caring must always take place in the context of being careful.

Understanding Danger

Danger in this context refers to any condition or life situation that has the potential for exposing children to harm. Consequently, life situations such as eating, talking, walking, bicycle riding, playing, and riding in a motor vehicle all pose varying degrees of danger.

If we were to generate a list of life situations within each of the seven centers of care, many of them would have the potential for causing harm to the participants. Even the aging process, a life condition to which all human beings are exposed, is not without danger. As we age, our risk of experiencing age-related diseases and illnesses increases. Life is finite; death will eventually come to all living things.

Again, let me reemphasize that the goal is not to scare children regarding the existence of danger but to help them live full and complete lives knowing that danger, once understood, can be effectively managed. The good news is that all children can experience full lives and increase their safety when they are aware of and responsive to the dangers in their midst. Children who understand danger and how to lower their risk are less likely to place themselves in harm's way.

Danger in My Midst

Children and adults are exposed to dangers in their homes, schools, and communities. They are likewise exposed to global dangers, interpersonal dangers, seasonal dangers, recreational dangers, health-related dangers, natural disasters, and so on. Danger is inescapable. The best way to deal with danger is to challenge it head-on.

Home, School, and Community Dangers

As human beings, we are exposed to dangers where we live. Children experience life in their homes, schools, and communities. Dangers in the home relate to the potential for fires, electrical shock, falls, accidental poisoning, and air-quality problems that can compromise health and cause death (radon, allergens, carbon monoxide, natural gas).

School environments present similar dangers to those experienced in the home, but one can add to this list playground injuries, interpersonal conflicts, fights, shootings, and bullying. Schools are like mini-communities and present many of the same dangers seen in towns, villages, and cities.

Community dangers include, but are not limited to, such factors as racial and ethnic unrest, poverty, unemployment, poor housing, racial discrimination, prejudices, injustices and inequities, illness and disease, exposure to natural disasters, and terrorism. Communities must strive to understand these dangers and work to lower the probability of their occurrence.

Global Dangers

Global dangers are those life conditions and situations that expose large numbers of people and the ecosystem to harm. They emerge as a result of the careless action and inaction of people and through natural disasters over which people have limited control. Some examples of global dangers to which children are exposed are: the sun's radiation due to a decrease in the ozone layer, volcanic eruptions, mudslides, earthquakes, tornadoes, hurricanes, floods, and forest fires. Other global dangers involve pollution of our environment, depletion of natural resources, wars between nations, terrorism, poverty, and illness. All of these global dangers are intensified when human beings fail to make caring choices that reduce their exposure and the exposure of others to unnecessary harm.

Interpersonal Dangers

Interpersonal dangers are those dangers that escalate between and among people who are unable to, or who fail to, resolve conflicts over resources, needs and wants, and beliefs and values. Interpersonal dangers can arise between two or more people, between groups of people, and among people in the same group. When conflicts escalate tempers flare, fists fly, and weapons are used. Interpersonal dangers can be reduced when people learn how to care for themselves and others in the context of being careful.

Seasonal/Environmental Dangers

The four seasons of the year present their own set of dangers. Winter months expose children to snow, ice, freezing rain, slippery streets and walks, and a host of winter sports and activities that have the potential of causing harm. Specific winter-related dangers are heart attacks, muscle strains, slips and falls, head injuries, broken bones, hypothermia, home fires, and vehicular crashes, all possibly producing injuries or death.

The remaining three seasons of the year expose children and adults to outdoor dangers emanating from such activities as bicycling, walking, boating, hunting, fishing, swimming, hiking, mowing lawns, sunbathing, farming, and outdoor sports. Many of the injuries and deaths from seasonal dangers are preventable when children practice helpful, caring strategies that lower their risk to harm.

Recreational Dangers

Many of the recreational dangers have been addressed under previous categories of danger. Some additional recreational activities that pose a danger to children are water and snow skiing, sledding, spelunking, school and summer league sports, tennis, and so on. Recreational dangers are also manageable if they are understood and addressed accordingly.

Health Dangers

Children are exposed to health-related dangers when they smoke or are around people who do. Their health is further compromised if they consume alcohol, drugs, eat unhealthy foods, gain excessive weight, or live sedentary lifestyles. Children who do not care for themselves or who make careless health-related choices increase their exposure to stress, hypertension, cardiovascular disease, type 2 diabetes, compromised immune systems, communicable diseases, and related damage to all body systems brought on by physical, mental, and emotional abuse.

While dangers like those mentioned give cause for concern, they need not cause alarm. Children can learn to manage the dangers to which they, others, and the environment are exposed by taking time to care and be careful. Children who give and receive care are changed by their experiences and in turn help others to change as well. The goal of caregivers and receivers of care is to increase safety and decrease dangers to self, others, and the environment by participating in a circle of care in which personal freedom is gained through responsible action. For this goal to become a reality, children must become aware of and understand the relationship between caring and danger. These two elements are thoroughly intertwined.

Identifying Danger

Children must be able to detect the presence of danger before they can respond to it. If they understand that danger is always in their midst, they are more likely to approach all life situations from a caring perspective that includes being careful.

As children learn to scan their environment, using their five senses, they will become more aware of themselves, others, and the world in which they live. We want children first to understand that danger is ever present, in all life situations and experiences. While it is not always visible, it is always there. Secondly, we want children to recognize that while all actions once taken, and their consequences, are final, they begin as choices to be considered. Choices have consequences, and it is in the consequences that danger lies. For example, you are walking with a friend next to a riverbank. Neither of you can swim. Your friend slips and falls into the river. What do you do? If you view this life situation in terms of the dangers involved, your goal is to help your friend without placing yourself or your friend in needless danger. You now see a number of choices open to you. You can throw a flotation object to your friend; call for help; or climb down the river bank, hold onto a tree, and extend a leg or stick for your friend to grab. These options offer help to your friend while neither placing him in more danger or exposing yourself to unnecessary danger. Not seeing these options, you might have jumped into the water to save your friend and become involved in a double drowning.

Children have the capacity to reduce their exposure to danger if they see and pay attention to the warning signs. With training, children can be taught how to use their five senses of smell, sight, hearing, touch, and taste, as well as their ability to reason, in reducing their exposure to danger.

Children can learn about the dangers associated with eating, such as choking, overeating, and the effects of a high-fat, high-sugar diet on health. Armed with this understanding, children can modify their behavior by eating slowly and chewing their food so that it can be swallowed safely. They can monitor their daily calorie intake, eat in moderation, and select a high-fiber diet rich in lean meat, fruits, and vegetables. They can learn about the dangers associated with a sedentary lifestyle and choose to exercise daily—in moderation and with caution so as not to hurt themselves. They likewise can learn about the dangers and early warning signs of various diseases and illnesses, and choose prevention involving lifestyle modifications, regular doctor visits, and self-observation routines. They can learn about the effects of hypertension, cardiovascular disease, diabetes, and cancer on the body, They can also learn about the preventive choices they can make to care for themselves, including early detection measures that will help them live longer and healthier lives.

Children need opportunities to identify signs of danger and perceive what they can do to prevent it when possible and lower their risk when it is inescapable. For example, children, when entering a building, should recognize the potential dangers of fire, bomb threats, terrorism, and natural disasters. They should locate safety evacuation instructions, exit signs, and stairways that they can use in the event of an emergency situation that requires them to leave the building quickly and safely. Children can use their sense of smell and touch (warning signs) to indicate the presence of fire. Once armed with this information, they need to know what they can do to protect themselves in a burning building filled with smoke and dangerous fumes.

Children seeing dark clouds and lightning, and experiencing high winds should understand these warning signs and how to respond to them. Children should likewise understand such warning signs and signals as horns, sirens, flashing red lights, whistles, road markings, crosswalks, railroad crossing gates, vehicular and pedestrian traffic control devices, smoke detectors, flares, and bodily warning signs (temperature, high blood-pressure readings, sore throat, pain, etc.) and how to respond to them in caring and responsible ways.

Children must also learn how to identify danger in their relationships with others. Anger is often identified through raised voices, clenched fists, flushed skin, erratic and nervous behavior, tense muscles, and voice inflection, as well as through words themselves. All of these warning signs signal potential conflict and physical harm. Understanding these warning signs is a prerequisite to safe, caring, and careful actions that are required to defuse a potentially dangerous situation.

Danger signs and their significance take on additional meaning in the context of the environment in which they are observed. For example, loaded guns at a firing range are of less concern than loaded guns seen in a school building. Medications in a hospital being administered by qualified medical personnel pose less of a danger than uncontrolled substances on a school playground.

Children need to be alert to suspicious behaviors and warning signs, and ready to report what they have observed, making caring and careful choices that can save lives. Early detection of danger in homes, schools, communities, and globally is a first step that children can take in preventing and combating the potential effects of danger while increasing safety through responsible caring.

Danger and the Seven Centers of Care

Danger is ever present in the life choices that children make. As indicated in chapter 2, all the choices that children will ever make will be in the seven centers of care. Consequently, all dangers to which children will ever be exposed can be found in the seven centers of care as well. Therefore, we want children to be sensitive to the fact that caring is not without danger. Caring must always take place in the context of being careful. Hidden in the consequences of every life choice are the dangers associated with the life situation or condition being experienced or about to be experienced.

What follows is a brief discussion of each of the seven centers of care and a few examples of the potential dangers associated with each. Chapter 4 sensitizes the reader to the connection between caring and danger; chapter 5 will focus on how children can live full and reasonably safe lives by learning how to be careful when caring for themselves, others, and the environment.

Caring for Self

When children fail to care for themselves or care in ways that are not based on Right, Reality, and Responsibility, they subject themselves, others, and the environment to danger. Many children are unaware of the dangers that surround them, or are aware of them but do not possess the self-protective factors needed to care for themselves. Others simply ignore the dangers, hoping that they will not be affected by them (wishful thinking). Specific dangers associated with harmful self-care actions are the following:

- Unintentional injuries (injuries that occur from accidents, conflicts, diseases, illnesses, poor health choices, etc.)
- Intentional injuries (suicide, homicide, fighting, self-inflicted injuries)
- Compromised health states resulting from the use of drugs, alcohol, and tobacco products
- Infections, communicable diseases, pregnancies, sexually transmitted diseases
- Health dangers associated with poor nutrition, eating disorders, and obesity
- Health dangers associated with limited or absence of physical activity
- Depression
- Lowered self-esteem
- Stress
- Violence.

These dangers can be reduced significantly when children are aware of and understand the dangers and warning signs associated with harmful self-care choices.

Caring for Family and Friends

The goal of caring for family and friends is to establish healthful relationships that encourage cooperation, inclusion, independence, personal growth, and community building. Destructive and hurtful relations emerge when family and friends ignore, are unaware of, do not understand, or fail to respond in caring and careful ways to the potential dangers that are present in all relationships. Some of the following harmful actions are likely to emerge when family and friends cease to care in the context of being careful:

- Unjust criticism
- Put-downs
- Manipulation based on fear and guilt
- Name calling
- Conflict and discrimination
- Misuse and abuse of alcohol and drugs
- Helplessness
- Conditional love
- Overprotection
- Reinforcement of counterproductive behavior
- Distrust and loss of respect
- Power struggles
- Withdrawal
- Displays of anger and isolation.

These dangers and others like them need not destroy interpersonal relationships if children are aware of and understand that giving and receiving care is risky business. Relationship building is a mutual caring experience in which caregivers and receivers of care share equally in the connections that are being forged. Therefore, they must work together in reducing the dangers that threaten their union.

Caring for Acquaintances and Distant Others

When children and adults cease to care for acquaintances and distant others, they widen the gap between themselves and people on whom they must rely for their own care. The reality is that much of the care we receive comes from people we do not know. Humankind will truly be in danger when people stop caring for acquaintances and distant others. The life lesson that is crucial for children to learn with respect to caring is that trust, safety, security, and a sense of belonging are by-products of a caring, global community. In the absence of a caring community, children are likely to experience more prejudice, discrimination, oppression, and social inequities, which tend to create social unrest, civil disobedience, conflict, injury, and loss of life. These are the real dangers, and they emerge when people cease to care beyond their own inner circle.

To do nothing to promote the fair treatment of all human beings serves to condone mistreatment and social injustice. Such mistreatment and unfair practices related to issues of gender, age, race, socioeconomic class, religion, and disabilities widen the gaps between human beings and escalate the danger of disruption and destruction of the very fabric on which our country was founded—equality and the freedom to pursue one's dreams.

Danger growing out of a failure to act will not go away on its own, nor will the destructive impact of danger subside, until action is taken to correct what divides diverse people. Caring is the cosmic glue that binds people of diversity together. However, caring itself is not without danger. Wars have been fought in the name of caring; law enforcement personnel have lost their lives fighting for social justice; and people have lost their jobs, friends, and families acting on their beliefs and values regarding what is legally, ethically, and morally the right thing to do.

While caring for acquaintances and distant others involves danger, not caring poses the greater danger. We want children to recognize the importance of being careful while caring. We also want them to exercise the courage of their convictions to speak the truth and act powerfully in their quest to become caring human beings and builders of caring communities.

Caring for Nonhuman Animals

Caring for pets, domestic animals, and animals of the wild is something we want children to do. However, the manner in which children care for animals is critical, for animals pose a danger to human beings. Ensuring the safety of people and animals must therefore guide the caring process at all times.

Animals have caused human suffering, injury, and death when human beings have failed to consider the dangers. Consequently, even well-intentioned and caring human beings have been attacked, bitten, mauled, and killed by animals (pets, domestic, and wild) because they failed to "play it safe."

Despite how cute, playful, and docile animals may appear to be, their behavior is not always predicable. Animals are very territorial, instinctual by nature, and responders by virtue of their genetic makeup. They are wired for survival; anything that threatens or disrupts their survival mode is provocation for action. Sudden movement; changes in scent, hunger, illness; or anything that threatens their safety or that of their young can quickly set off a chain reaction of events the consequences of which are often inescapable.

Danger exists when feeding and watering animals, administering medical treatment, tagging animals for study, treating an animal in pain, and transporting animals from one location to another. People are also at risk when they enter animal habitats during periods of migration, mating, and giving birth. When children fail to understand the nature of animals and do not heed their warning signs, they increase their exposure to harm.

While animals (pets, domestic, and wild) present a danger to human beings, human beings may place animals and the public in danger as well. Human beings present a danger to animals and the public when they:

- Pollute the natural environment
- Abuse hunting and fishing laws
- Disobey governmental laws for the protection of endangered species
- Destroy wetlands and other animal habitats
- Illegally import and sell wild animals as pets
- Fail to license and inoculate pets
- Slaughter animals for their hides, tusks, shells, and so on
- Mistreat animals by providing poor living conditions
- Misuse and abuse animals using harmful training methods
- Practice unsafe preparation and packaging of meat and fish for market.

Consequently, we want children to recognize that caring for animals is not without danger. However, learning to care for animals in the context of being careful will enable them to appreciate fully the value of animals and what they can do to help maintain a circle of care in which they and the animals they love benefit from the care that each has to give.

Caring for Plants and the Physical Environment

Children must learn to be careful when caring for plants and the physical environment. For example, some plants are poisonous to consume, while others are harmful to touch, causing rashes and irritation to

the skin. Some plants, while beautiful to behold, choke desired vegetation, destroy wetlands, and negatively impact the quality of lakes and
ponds. Also, some plants are illegal to grow in this country and else-
where in the world because they are used to make illicit drugs.

Plants and trees are sometimes placed in danger by those who care
for them. Too much or too little water can injure plants. Not using the
right kinds of fertilizers and plant nutrients can also place plants in danger as well. When children and adults destroy plants or unwisely cut
down too many trees, they create additional dangers that impact the environment and all life forms. Soil erosion; loss of shelter and habitats for
animals, insects, and birds; and increased exposure to solar radiation are
a direct result of careless actions that can cause devastating harmful
effects.

Plants and trees replenish oxygen and help purify the air we breathe.
They are a source of food for all living creatures, and they provide medicines used to treat a variety of diseases and illnesses. These benefits too
are threatened by people who fail to recognize how careless actions disrupt the balance of nature. When plants and trees are destroyed, they
can no longer provide the care that nature intended.

Our physical environment, while a joy to experience, also presents
dangers of its own. Natural disasters (hurricanes, tornadoes, fires,
floods, landslides, avalanches, volcanoes, earthquakes, and hail, ice, and
snowstorms) injure and kill thousands of people every year. When people understand and respond responsibly to the warning signs that signal
danger, bodily injury and needless loss of life can be greatly curtailed.

Air, soil, and water pollution and the unwise use of natural resources
create additional dangers to our planet and to ourselves. Very few young
people set out to pollute the environment, yet we are experiencing a reduction in the earth's ozone layer, poor air quality in some parts of the
world, soil erosion, and the gradual destruction of natural parks and
recreation areas. Global warming and the gradual melting of global ice
fields present additional dangers to planet Earth, the effects of which
are currently being studied to determine the severity of the problem,
potential dangers, and what we can do to care for our home.

The physical characteristics of our environment present formidable
challenges to some who long to test themselves against the natural elements. Rock and mountain climbers, snowboarders and skiers, scuba

divers, dirt bikers, white-water rafters and kayakers, hikers, bicyclists, and hunters are exposed to environmental dangers while endangering the very environment that many of these people seek to enjoy and strive to protect.

Every year, people are injured and killed while enjoying the physical environment because they were unaware of the dangers or were not adequately prepared to deal with them. Every year desert plants and sea grasses are destroyed, underwater plants and reefs are damaged, mineral formations in caves are broken, and parks and recreation areas are damaged by people who enjoy the physical environment but fail to care for it. Caring for the physical environment is not without danger for those who speak out to protect it, pass laws to care for it better, and who require the public to take special training and classes to protect and enjoy it.

We want children to enjoy the physical environment and to experience the care which it provides to those who care for it. Rather than become unsuspecting victims of the environment, we want children to care and to be careful while enjoying the physical environment and protecting it for others to enjoy as well. Lastly, we want children to understand that life's dangers lay hidden in the consequences of their actions. Awareness of this fact is a prerequisite to becoming a formidable risk manager and a responsible caregiver.

Caring for the Human-Made World of Objects and Instruments

All objects and instruments designed to benefit humankind also have the potential for placing people in harm's way. Bicycles, clothing, radios, toys, seat belts, computers, homes, and pencils all have a dangerous side. When children misuse objects and instruments, fail to store them properly, do not keep them in good repair, and fail to comply with manufacturer's recommendations for their care and use, they place themselves and others in danger.

When manufacturers produce objects and instruments with defects, make false claims, and fail to test properly the safety of their products, they place the public in danger. Safety-minded people place themselves in danger when they speak out against these products and have them removed from store shelves. However, these people, because they had the courage to care, reduce the danger and improve the safety of others.

Many children have become the victims of objects and instruments designed to improve the quality of their lives. Medicines, clothing, toys, bedding, and vehicular child-safety seats have been the subject of discussion in recent years because of the dangers associated with some of them.

We want children to recognize that despite all the good brought by objects and instruments, they must be used with due care because of the harm that can come to those who fail to be careful. This caution is especially important because children live in a world that embraces technology. Something that is so prevalent and commonplace can be easily taken for granted and the harm that can occur overlooked. Herein lies the danger—no object or instrument is completely safe.

Objects and instruments also impact the remaining six centers of care and effect every dimension of a child's being (physical, emotional, social, intellectual, and spiritual). They have the potential of damaging children's health, their relationships with others, animal life, plants and the environment, and the shaping and transporting of harmful ideas. Therefore, our goal as educators must be one of teaching children the importance of caring and being careful when using objects and instruments. We want them to respect their potential for doing good while being alert to the potential dangers in their use and care.

Caring for Ideas

Children live in a society of ideas. Ideas play a powerful role in their lives. They shape their very being and give their lives purpose and meaning. Ideas guide them in their pursuit of basic goodness and a life of caring and community building.

In the absence of caring ideas, children will lose their way, community building will falter, and society will lose its focus in promoting justice for all. Caring ideas are needed in today's world because: they bring people together; support inclusion, cooperation, and peacemaking; and instill a commitment in people to stand up for what is legally, ethically, and morally right.

Caring for ideas worthy of care comes with a cost. People must be willing to give of their time, talent, and treasure in support of basic goodness. Caring for caring ideas also can be dangerous; people have lost friendships, been ridiculed, harassed, physically harmed, and killed for standing up for what is right. Caring is not always an easy thing to do. It takes courage to care for those who may need care, and to care for those whom we do not know.

Caring ideas give children direction in sorting out right from wrong, but they may not give them the courage to act. Teaching children about the Golden Rule (treating others as you would like to be treated) does not prepare them to intervene when other children are being teased, ridiculed, bullied, or mistreated in some way. There is danger in such action and a price to be paid in caring for ideas that have value.

As educators, we can help children to learn about whistle blowers, politicians, environmental protectionists, and champions of human rights who stood their ground in support of ideas that have improved the quality of their lives. These people learned to say "yes" in the face of fear and acted in the presence of danger to provide care in the centers of care.

We want children to understand that not all ideas are caring ideas and that some ideas can be very dangerous. Ideas that support racism, classism, sexism, ageism, handicapism, and religious oppression are discriminatory and prejudicial in nature. These ideas disrupt community building, divide people of diversity, and create conflict and dissention. These ideas and ones like them pose a danger to people who support a democratic way of life.

Ideas that promote inequities in income, housing, health care, and safety are as dangerous as those that encourage the destruction of our environment. We want children to understand that danger accompanies dangerous ideas. We also want them to understand that caring for caring ideas is not without danger either. To do nothing in the presence of harmful ideas escalates the danger to those who are impacted by these ideas. The only way to reduce danger is to diminish the existence of harmful ideas while promoting worthy ideas deserving of our care. Ideas that are based on Right, Reality, and Responsibility care for people and communities that care.

ROLE OF FACILITATOR

Your role, as facilitator, is to help children become aware of and to understand the nature of danger. Danger speaks to one's personal exposure to harm. Harm can be physical as well as emotional. You want children to recognize that nothing in life is completely safe. There is always an element of danger associated with every action. Your goal in sharing this insight with children is not to scare them but rather to help them to care more deeply, manage risk more responsibly, and live life more fully, better prepared to recognize and deal effectively with dangers in their midst.

You want your children to understand that their lives have value and that because they have value, it is important that they do not endanger them. By learning about the dangers in the seven centers of care, children will be able to care and be careful in support of themselves, others, and the planet.

Learning about danger is not an excuse for children to recoil from life but rather to experience fully life's challenges knowing that they can do so in a climate of safety. Danger is a given. It is not something to hide from children as a way of protecting them. Indeed, we expose children to more harm when we keep from them life's simple truths, one of which is that danger is most effectively addressed when we are aware of its presence.

Throughout this chapter, your children will gain practice in identifying dangers in the seven centers of care. They will understand the harm that can come in each center when people cease to care in the context of being careful.

Your children will be challenged to identify dangers in their homes, schools, communities, and in their world. They will examine interpersonal relationships and the dangers that abound. They will also explore seasonal, recreational, and health dangers to which they are exposed.

As your children come to understand the nature of danger, they will learn about the signs, signals, sounds, control devices, and related instruments and objects that warn of danger and how to respond safely in response to these warnings. Also, they will be taught how to rely on their five senses in identifying the presence of danger.

Teach your children that danger also lurks in the consequences of their actions. If they take time to examine the consequences of their actions prior to acting, they will decrease the danger to which they are exposed. In chapter 3 they learned about helpful and hurtful habits. Revisit this chapter and discuss with your children habits that increase their exposure to danger and those that increase their safety. Because habits are automatic, children are not likely to examine the consequences of their actions prior to acting. Taking time to help children examine their habits provides a pause for reflection and contemplation, as well as an opportunity to make life changes that will increase their safety.

Again, your purpose is not to frighten your children but to teach them to become detectives and "super sleuths" in search of potential dangers in the seven centers of care. Awareness of danger is children's first defense against becoming victims. Once your children are able to spot danger, they will be ready to participate fully in chapter 5 activities, which focus on teaching children to be careful.

Have fun teaching your children that learning how to be careful begins with their ability to identify danger in the world. Armed with this skill, your children will be another step closer to becoming caring human beings and builders of caring communities.

BENEFITS TO CHILDREN

Children who understand the relationship between caring and danger:

- Recognize that caring and danger are inseparable
- Increase their awareness of danger
- Pay attention to the warning signs of danger
- Make caring choices in the context of being careful.

PITFALLS TO CHILDREN

Children who fail to understand the relationship between caring and danger:

- Lack awareness regarding the presence of danger
- Miss the warning signs that signal danger
- Make caring choices in the absence of being careful
- Place themselves, others, and the environment in danger.

ACTIVITIES

Super Sleuth

Objectives

1. To help children understand the meaning of danger
2. To help children identify examples of danger.

Group Size: Classroom group
Time: 15 to 30 minutes
Materials: None needed
Facilitator: This activity will help children understand that danger relates to their personal exposure to harm. Most, if not all, life experiences pose some degree of danger; few things in life are completely safe. In this activity, you will be teaching your children about danger as well as increasing their awareness of it. You will be helping them understand that their first defense against danger is to become aware of it, which will increase their ability to reduce their exposure to it.

Process

1. Explain to your children that danger relates to their exposure to harm, injury, or loss. For someone to be in danger means that they are in harm's way.
2. Explain to your children that people, animals, plants, and the environment can experience danger, in that they are all vulnerable to harm.
3. To help your children understand better the definition of danger, write the following life situations on the chalkboard: riding a bicycle, eating in the cafeteria, playing outside, and walking down the hall.
4. Explain to your children that all of the above situations present some degree of danger (harm). For each life situation listed, ask your children to become detectives and name possible dangers they or others could experience.
5. Once your children understand the meaning of danger, ask them to name one possible danger for each of the following experiences:

walking on a frozen pond, touching an electric fence, calling someone a name, riding in a car, cooking food, and not turning in school
work.

6. Encourage your children to add additional life situations (experiences) to the above list and have them function as super sleuths,
uncovering hidden dangers in their midst.

Discussion

1. Have your children define the meaning of danger.
2. Ask them why it is important for them to be aware of danger.
3. Encourage your children to discuss examples of danger that relate
to things they enjoy doing, like swimming, playing baseball, listening to music, and so on.

Homework

1. Ask your children to collect pictures from magazines that depict
various life situations. Show the pictures and have your children
identify the possible dangers depicted.
2. Have your children bring in newspaper articles that describe examples of danger. Discuss these articles in class.
3. Ask your children to look for examples of potential danger at
home, on the playground, at the mall, and in their community.
Have them bring their lists to class and show what they have discovered (super sleuths).

Name That Danger

Objective: To help children identify danger in the seven centers of
care.

Group Size: Classroom group, two teams

Time: 15 to 30 minutes

Materials: seven stacks of three-by-five index cards, stopwatch, timer,
or watch with a second hand

Facilitator: "Name That Danger" is a card game that will help children to
become familiar with examples of danger in the seven centers of care.

Process

1. Divide your class into two teams.
2. Provide your children with the following directions: "Today we are going to play a card game called 'Name That Danger.' I have seven stacks of cards that present life situations in each of the seven centers of care. I will flip a coin to determine which group begins. I will then draw a card from stack 1 and read it to the first group. The group, working together, will have 15 seconds to Name That Danger. One point will be earned for each correct response. I will then draw a card from stack 2 and repeat the process for team 2. The game will be played for 10 minutes. After 10 minutes, the points will be totaled. The object of the game is for each team to earn as many points as it can."
3. What follows are some life situation suggestions for each center of care. Each life situation presents one or more dangers for your children to name:
   - Caring for self: eating candy, listening to music, swimming, getting angry, and sunbathing
   - Caring for intimate others (family and friends): doing your friends' homework, lying, getting angry with a friend or family member, telling others what to do, cutting ahead of others in line, not listening to others
   - Caring for acquaintances and distant others: sticking up for someone who is being teased, giving money to charity, reporting a crime, asking a person you don't know for help, telling racial or ethnic jokes, treating people disrespectfully, doing nothing to stop bullying
   - Caring for nonhuman animals: playing with a pet, feeding animals at the zoo, failing to water and feed animals, shooting animals who are in danger of extinction, failing to license a pet, and failing to get your pet shots
   - Caring for plants and the environment: walking in the woods, picking plants in the woods, cutting down trees, throwing trash from your car window, burning leaves, going mountain climbing, failing to heed storm warnings
   - Caring for objects and instruments: playing a car radio, mowing the lawn with a power mower, using firearms, reading books, us-

ing a computer to get information, tipping back in your chair, and inflating a bicycle tire

- Caring for ideas: honesty is the best policy, be kind to everyone, some people are better than others, all ideas are good ideas, stand up for what you believe in, and speak out against acts of racial prejudice.

Discussion

1. Help your children to understand that caring is not without danger. Most acts of caring have some danger.
2. Have your children discuss some of the dangers present in many caring professions. Discuss some of the dangers that doctors, rescue workers, military personnel, teachers, miners, farmers, and other workers face daily in their work.
3. Ask your children if they believe that they and others should stop caring for themselves, others, or the environment knowing that caring can be dangerous.
4. Remind your children that while caring does expose them to danger (seven centers of care), they can learn to be careful when caring. Tell them that they will learn how to be careful in chapter 5 of this program.
5. Explain to your children that while there is some danger in caring, not to care is even more dangerous. Ask them what life would be like at home, in their classrooms, in their communities, and throughout the world if everyone stopped caring.

Homework

1. Ask your children to think about ways they can reduce danger in their lives. Give them a list of five life situations and ask them to identify a danger for each and one thing they could do to reduce that danger. For example: Walking down the hall $->$ bumping into someone $->$ Walk on the right side of the hallway.
2. Ask your children to discuss with family members some things they can do to reduce danger and increase their safety when making caring choices.

These two homework assignments will prepare children to better understand how danger can be addressed when people are aware of its existence.

Danger Signs and Senses

Objectives: To help children identify danger signs using their senses.
Group Size: Classroom group or small work groups (4 people per group)
Time: 15 to 30 minutes
Materials: None needed
Facilitator: This activity will help children identify signs of danger using their five senses. You will be helping children understand how they reduce their risk of danger by being more aware of its presence.

Process

1. Explain to your children that people who recognize signs of danger, know what they mean and how to respond to them can make caring choices while reducing their risk of being harmed.
2. Tell your children that they will be learning to use their five senses to identify signs of danger. Sights, sounds, smells, taste, and touch provide useful information in helping to keep children out of harm's way. Explain to your children the importance of their five senses and how they can be used by sharing with them the examples that follow:
   • Sight: Your sight will help you to identify danger signs that are observable. Traffic signal lights, flashing lights, railroad crossing gates, written signs, thermometers, blood-pressure gauges, and automobile warning gauges are just a few of the many visual signs that warn of danger. You can also detect interpersonal dangers by observing nonverbal signs, such as clenched fists, rigid postures, and red faces that signal anger or conflict. Discuss visual signs of danger and others not mentioned here. Have your children identify various careers that depend on visual signs of danger and how these warning signs help reduce harm and increase safety.

- Sound: Your hearing will help you to be alert to danger as well. Some examples of auditory warning signs are sirens, whistles, alarms, bells, bodily sounds (heartbeats, blood pressure, breathing), thoughts, words, and so on. Discuss the many sounds that warn of danger and the various careers that use sound as warning signs. Also, have your children note how they can combine the use of their sight and hearing to increase their detection of danger.

- Smell: Odors provide additional information that warn of danger. Some examples of smells that alert people to possible harm are smoke, spoiling food, changes in body odor, and poisonous substances that have distinctive smells. Discuss with your children the importance of smell and how various odors can be signs of danger. Discuss various careers that rely on detecting various smells in keeping people from being harmed. Challenge your children to combine sight, sound, and smell in better detecting signs of danger.

- Touch: Signs of danger can also be detected though your sense of touch and physical feelings that you experience. Some examples are pain (physical and emotional), and changes in body temperature, blood pressure, and stress. Touch can be used to detect hot and cold, texture, and changes in pressure. Discuss with your children how touch and physical sensations can warn them of danger. Discuss various professions that rely on the use of touch to detect signs of danger.

- Taste: Your taste buds can detect signs of danger as well. Some taste sensations are a sign of illness in the body. Taste can be used to detect food that is not properly cooked and identify change in familiar foods or medicines that might indicate the addition of substances that could be harmful. Be sure to caution your children about using their sense of taste in ways that could subject them to additional harm. In other words, they should not taste things that are unfamiliar to them.

3. Explain to your children the value of using all of their senses together when identifying signs of danger. Demonstrate this by having them explain the different senses they would use in detecting fire, an impending storm, anger or conflict, and illness.

4. Have your children identify warning signs of danger in each of the seven centers of care using their five senses:
   • Caring for self: physical health warning signs, emotional health warning signs, and educational warning signs
   • Caring for intimate others (family and friends): social (interpersonal) warning signs
   • Caring for acquaintances and distant others: community building warning signs (threats to community building)
   • Caring for nonhuman animals: warning signs that communicate danger to animals and warning signs that signal danger to people
   • Caring for the human-made world of objects and instruments: warning signs that indicate that objects and instruments pose a danger, and objects and instruments that are designed to warn of danger
   • Caring for ideas: ideas that signal danger and warning signs that alert people to dangerous ideas.

Discussion

1. Ask your children how they can use their five senses to warn them of danger.
2. Have your children describe how animals and insects use their senses to warn them of danger.
3. With all of the different warning signs that exist, ask your children to explain why they believe so many children and adults are harmed (injured and killed) every year.

Homework

Ask your children to practice using their five senses at home, in school, and in their communities to detect signs of danger. Make a list of the warning signs they identify and the senses they use to make their discoveries. For example, children might study what cars and drivers do when they approach a stop sign. Children observe that 25 percent of the cars come to a complete stop, while 75 percent slow down but drive through the intersection. The visual sign of danger is the number of motorists who drive through stop signs. Given this new information, children should wait for cars to come to a complete stop, look both ways, and then cross the street.

Devices That Warn of Danger

Objectives

1. To help children name (identify) devices that warn of danger
2. To help children understand how these devices warn of danger and what they must do to care for themselves.

Group Size: Classroom group or small work groups (two or three children)

Time: 15 to 30 minutes

Materials: "Devices That Warn and What to Do" handout (handout 4.1) and a few objects and instruments that warn of danger.

Facilitator: This activity helps children to identify various devices that warn of danger and how they can reduce the threat of danger by using them. Help them understand that their bodies contain a variety of warning systems that if used will help them to avoid serious harm to themselves.

Process

1. Discuss with your children various bodily functions that warn of danger as well as medical objects and instruments that help to detect danger. X-rays, blood-chemistry tests, small cameras that can be swallowed, magnetic and sound imaging technology, and various types of scopes and gauges (blood pressure, eye pressure, thermometers) can detect early body warning signs, resulting in early prevention measures or early treatment. Today, there are many detectable early warning signs for a variety of illnesses and diseases. Early detection leads to prevention and less invasive treatment options. Explain to your children how they can benefit from regular physical, eye, ear, and dental exams. Prevention and early detection of health problems are possible when warning signs are discovered early. The best and most effective health insurance available to children is what they do to care for themselves in the context of being careful.
2. Refer your children to handout 4.1. Ask them to list devices that warn of danger and then actions they can take in response to the warning. Give your children three to five minutes to complete this activity.

3. Ask your children to share their list of devices that warn of danger and how they would respond to the warning.

4. Show your children a variety of devices that warn of danger. Explain that these devices must be kept in good working condition and that they must be used if they are to provide the warning (care) they were meant to offer.

Discussion

Discuss situations in which warning devices have not helped people increase their safety. Provide some reasons as to why these devices may not have performed as expected. Three major reasons why warning signs may not reduce people's exposure to danger are that the warning devices are not properly maintained, people fail to use them, or people did not know how to use them.

Homework

Ask your children to make a list of all the devices in their world that warn of danger and what people must do to derive protection from their use. What follows is a partial list of devices that warn of danger:

- Flares
- Radios and television
- Railroad crossing gates, flashing lights, and bells
- Intersection traffic signals
- Road signs, road markings, and traffic control devices
- Poison control stickers
- Warning signs on medicines, tobacco products, and alcohol
- Automobile gauges
- Smoke and heat alarms
- Carbon monoxide detectors
- Sirens (police, emergency vehicles, ambulances)
- Circuit breakers and fuses
- Thermometers
- Blood-pressure monitors
- Tire gauges

- Nutritional information (food and beverage products)
- Overpass height signs
- Failing grades on papers
- Equipment instruction booklets
- Changing statistics (crime, illness, poverty, and so on)
- Weather gauges and reports
- Sensor strips that detect changes in chemistry (soil, body, and chemicals).

SUGGESTED ACTIVITIES FOR THE WEEK

Language Arts and Reading

Have your children read stories, write creative papers, and recite poems depicting caring and danger in the seven centers of care. They can also view movies and television news magazines that present life experiences that are full of adventure, danger, and adversity. Have your children discuss these life dramas and how they communicate caring and danger. Also explore with your children how reading, writing, and language skills are caring skills. These skills can be used by children to promote caring and being careful. These skills are often used to help people understand the nature of danger and how they can care for themselves, others, and the planet.

Math

Numbers play a major role in our lives. Children and adults depend on numbers in many different ways, one of which is to warn of danger. Explore with your children the many and varied ways in which numbers are used in this regard. For example, thermometers, blood-chemistry profiles, speedometers, and speed-limit signs all rely on numbers to warn of danger. Your children will be amazed at the different ways in which numbers are used to signal danger. Other examples include vehicle weight-limit signs on roads and bridges; signs indicating bridge, tunnel, and underpass heights; and measuring devices that communicate flood-stage levels. Involve your children in exploring the caring nature of numbers and how they warn of danger in the seven centers of care.

DEVICES THAT WARN AND WHAT TO DO

Device #1: _____

What to Do: _____

Device #2: _____

What to Do: _____

Device #3: _____

What to Do: _____

Device #4: _____

What to Do: _____

Device #5: _____

What to Do: _____

Device #6: _____

What to Do: _____

Device #7: _____

What to Do: _____

Device #8: _____

What to Do: _____

Device #9: _____

What to Do: _____

Device #10: _____

What to Do: _____

Science

Science provides knowledge, facts, truth, and principles pertaining to our physical world. Science helps children understand and care for themselves, others, and the planet. Scientific exploration has improved the quality of life that we have all come to enjoy. However, scientific investigations and inventions are not without risk. There are dangers associated with all acts of care. Space exploration, the development of new medicines, organ transplants, treatments for various diseases, and most technological advances have the potential for harm as well as good. Explore with your children the dangers involved in caring and the warning signs that must be heeded in relationship to the seven centers of care.

Social Studies

When human beings interact with each other, there is always the potential for danger. Society teaches children a variety of social skills so they can become caring people and builders of caring communities. Have your children identify and practice some of these skills. Listening, speaking one at a time, sharing, taking turns, using manners, giving constructive feedback, complimenting others, and negotiating and mediating differences are just a few of the many social skills that promote cooperation and inclusion between and among people of diversity.

Explain to your children the dangers that can occur during social interactions. Disagreements can easily escalate into anger or conflict in which people are physically or emotionally harmed. Danger occurs when social rules and social skills are not practiced. Danger also escalates with rising social problems like poverty, crime, drug and alcohol abuse, unemployment, and racial and ethnic tensions that create social division.

Help your children identify the social/interpersonal warning signs that communicate danger. Help them to use their senses to spot rising tension, anger, and social unrest so that caring methods of intervention and prevention can prevail and cooperation can be achieved or restored.

Health and Physical Education

Caring and danger are very much a part of health and physical education. Whenever children care for themselves, there is always potential for harm. Therefore, children's physical, emotional, social, intellectual, and spiritual dimensions of self are always vulnerable to harm with respect to their daily life choices. Therefore, it is important for you to help your children understand the importance of making caring self-choices in the context of being careful.

Explore with your children some of the dangers associated with caring for themselves and some of the warning signs on which they can rely to live a wellness lifestyle. For example, some physical warning signs are pain; fatigue; difficulty breathing; and changes in bowel habits, weight, temperature, vision, hearing, sleep habits, and appetite. Explain to your children that regular checkups will help them to monitor and maintain good health.

Emotional warning signs might include unexplained mood changes, difficulty managing anger, low self-esteem, thoughts of suicide, and so on. Social warning signs could include loss of friendships, lack of interest in others, loneliness, fighting, bullying or being bullied, and impaired or absent caring social skills. Intellectual warning signs often include a sudden drop in grades, failure to turn in class work assignments, impaired memory, difficulty with comprehension, and missed days of school. Spiritual warning signs consist of a loss of direction and purpose, boredom, low interest in daily activities, and so on.

Help your children identify health-related warning signs and things they can do to care for themselves using what they learn in health and physical education classes. Help your children to understand that their good health is dependent on caring and being careful in all seven centers of care.

TIPS FOR CAREGIVERS

Caring and danger are like "two peas in a pod." They exist together. Caring, by its nature, exposes children to danger in a world that can never be completely safe. You must therefore teach your children how to give and receive care in the context of being careful. Your goal is not to scare your children but to teach them a very simple truth. Danger is a fact of life. It is not something to be feared; however it must be respected and addressed in a responsible manner.

Your children's first defense in response to danger is to be aware of its presence and to learn the warning signs that signal that presence. While you are teaching your children about danger, they will be learning more about it in school as well. With awareness will come understanding about caring and danger, followed by responsible action that will prevent or reduce the threat of harm to givers and receivers of care. What follows are some activities and life situations that will help you to increase your children's awareness and understanding of danger so that they will be able to live full and meaningful lives, caring in the context of being careful.

1. Explain to your children the meaning of danger. (Danger relates to harm. When someone is in danger or is doing something dangerous, they are in harm's way. They may experience emotional or physical pain as well as the possibility of dying.)
2. Help your children to understand that all life experiences expose them to varying degrees of danger. Present the following life experiences to your children and discuss the potential dangers to which they could be exposed: riding a bicycle, exercising, walking down a school hallway, mowing the lawn, eating candy, and saying something mean to a friend.
3. Explain to your children that danger can be managed (prevented or reduced) when they are aware of is presence. For example, if children are aware of the dangers associated with bike riding, they can take steps to prevent or reduce the danger to which they are exposed. Have your children identify bike riding dangers and things they can do to manage those dangers.
4. For each life situation listed in activity 2, ask your children to restate one danger and then something they can do to prevent or reduce that danger.
5. Explore with your children life situations in which they participate when not in school. For each life situation, explore some of the dangers and what they can do to be careful. Here are some examples of out-of-school activities: playing sports, pouring hot water, eating snack foods, swimming, watching television, riding an all-terrain vehicle, washing dishes, and playing video games.
6. Explain to your children that there are dangers within each of the seven centers of care. Create a card game for your children to play. Prepare three-by-five index cards in which you write a variety of life situations for each center of care. Randomly pull cards from the

seven centers. For each card drawn, ask your children to "Name That Danger." Here are a few ideas:

- Caring for self: not brushing teeth, getting angry, taking a bath, going ice skating, listening to music
- Caring for family and friends: lying, telling others what to do, talking when others are talking, insisting that people wear their seat belts, doing what others tell you to do, getting into an argument with a friend
- Caring for acquaintances and distant others: giving money to charity, reporting a crime, sticking up for someone you see being teased, telling a racial or ethnic joke, opening your door to someone you don't know, giving someone in need a ride, caring for someone who is ill
- Caring for nonhuman animals: playing with pets, feeding or petting wild animals at the zoo, failing to license a pet, teasing a pet, helping an injured wild animal, keeping food in your tent, shooting animals that are in danger of extinction
- Caring for plants and the environment: walking in the woods, picking plants in the woods, throwing trash out of your car window, burning leaves, standing under a tree during a lightning and thunder storm, going boating
- Caring for objects and instruments: playing a car radio, using firearms, shooting off fireworks, tipping back in a chair, putting air in a tire, cutting food with a knife, lighting candles, crossing the street on a red light (for you)
- Caring for ideas: honesty is the best policy, be kind to everyone; do what you are told; speak out against prejudice; all ideas are good ideas; some people deserve more respect than others.

7. Explain to your children the importance of recognizing signs of danger. Danger signs warn people of possible harm so that they can exercise due care and avoid or reduce harm to themselves and others. For example, stop signs warn of danger at road intersections. If this warning sign is heeded, fewer people will be hurt (pedestrians and motorists).

8. Help your children to identify as many warning signs as they can. Tell them that warning signs can be identified using their five senses (sight, sound, smell, touch, and taste). Using the warning

signs below, ask your children what they can do to care for themselves (others and the environment). Here are a few bodily warning signs that children should recognize: physical pain (teeth, eyes,
ears, body), sadness, rashes, and fever. Here are some environmental warning signs: flares; radio and television news and
weather; traffic lights, road signs, and road markings; traffic con-
trols; poison-control stickers; warning messages on medicine, tobacco, and alcohol; gauges (tire, automobile, blood-pressure, and
so on); smoke and fire alarms; sirens (police, emergency vehicles,
and ambulance); circuit breakers and fuses; nutritional information on foods and beverages; failing grades on papers; and fire
warning signs (national and state parks). Explore with your children how words, numbers, and other symbols warn of danger.

9. Help your children to identify interpersonal danger. When peo-
   ple get together there is always the threat of danger (anger, dis-
   agreements, fighting, or violence). Have them identify some of
   these warning signs and what they can do. Some warning signs
   are experienced internally, while others are observable in the ac-
   tions and reactions of those present:
   • Raised voices, yelling
   • Clenched fists
   • Tight muscles and knotted stomach
   • A feeling of losing control
   • Red face
   • Confusion
   • Rapid heart rate
   • Words that communicate harm (threat)
   • Racing thoughts
   • Fear
   • Tension and dry mouth.

10. Help children to recognize that their purpose in life is to care and to
    be careful. Help them be careful by recognizing the presence of
    danger and balancing it with safety. Here are a few areas in their lives
    where striving for safety has its own reward and personal payoff:
    • Water safety
    • Animal safety
    • Sports safety

- Fire safety
- Pedestrian and traffic safety
- Personal safety (taking care of myself)
- Bicycle safety
- Lawn care safety
- Poison safety
- Eating safety
- Winter safety
- Weapons safety
- Farm safety
- Home safety.

11. One thing that you and your children can do to spot and reduce danger at home is to do a home safety check. Here is a sample list of some things to place on a home safety checklist (make sure the following items are safe, in good working order, and do not pose harm to anyone in your home):
    - Electrical and mechanical equipment
    - Door locks
    - Windows
    - Smoke and fire alarms
    - Carbon monoxide detectors
    - Medicines (labels, storage, expiration dates)
    - Appliances
    - Electrical outlets
    - Electrical wiring
    - Fire extinguishers
    - Posted fire escape route
    - Emergency phone numbers
    - Steps and hallways (clear of clutter).

Help your children to become aware of danger! Teach them about the value of warning signs and how to use them in staying out of harm's way.

5

LEARNING TO BE CAREFUL

DEFINITION

R*isk Management*: Risk is a variable condition relating to one's chance of experiencing loss, injury, or death when exposed to danger. Risk management is a decision-making process designed to prevent or reduce one's exposure to danger.

BACKGROUND INFORMATION

An important aspect of being a caring person is learning to be careful. As children learn to care, they must be ever mindful of the dangers to which they, others, and the environment are exposed. With awareness, children will learn about the variable nature of risk and what they can do to become caring and responsible risk managers.

Risk Taking

Risk refers to children's level of exposure to danger. Risk is a variable condition that can change in response to how it is managed. While all children are in danger when they ride bicycles, their risk to personal harm may vary. For example, Jane wears a protective helmet when she rides her bicycle. Nancy does not wear a helmet when riding her bike. While both children are in danger of receiving head injuries, Nancy is at greater risk of receiving a serious head injury than Jane.

Risk taking is a choice that children make when they participate in life situations that expose them to danger. Risk taking is a matter of choice in that children have options regarding how much risk they are willing to accept.

Risk taking should not be taken lightly, nor should it be feared. Rather, children need to be taught about the realities of danger, the assessment of risk, and how to choose risk-taking strategies that will allow them to care in the context of being careful.

Children must be reminded that risk taking is a normal part of life and living, and that it contributes to their learning and personal growth. Risk taking encourages children to move out of their comfort zone and experience life as it was meant to be experienced. Risk taking adds vitality, stimulation, and excitement to life. It is a motivating force that challenges children to pursue lives of interest, purpose, and meaning. In contrast, a life devoid of risk taking is often boring, routine, highly predictable, and unimaginative.

However necessary risk taking may be in developing a quality life, it must be approached with caution. A favorable balance needs to be achieved between foolhardy risk taking and responsible and calculated risk taking, with safety in mind. Otherwise that which is designed to help create a full and meaningful life could bring one's own demise.

Foolhardy risk taking is tantamount to playing a game of chance (gambling) where the stakes are high, the odds of winning are low, and the losses are devastating and often irreversible. When foolhardy risk takers lose, the cost is in terms of human suffering (loss of property, mental and physical pain, and death). In contrast, calculated and cautious risk taking is controlled by the risk taker, and the results often lead to success in a climate of caring and safety.

The goal of chapter 5 is to encourage children to become caring and careful risk takers who have the courage to pursue lives of purpose and meaning. We want them to become responsible risk managers who value themselves, others, and the environment, and who care deeply about making the world a more caring and safer place to live.

How Children View Risk Taking

Children's perceptions of danger and risk will affect their behavior and the outcomes that emanate from their actions. Children who are taught to fear danger will fear life and will withdraw from it. Children who are given the courage, freedom, and opportunity to take risks in a supportive and nurturing climate will grow and learn from their experiences. They will achieve a sense of independence, industry, and accomplishment.

Some children are fearlessly optimistic and seemingly natural-born risk takers who are ready to try anything. They feel invincible and fully insulated from life's dangers. These children are often impulsive responders who act without thinking. They fail to see the danger in their midst and open themselves, others, and the environment to unnecessary risk.

The fearless and the fearful are at risk of experiencing loss, injury, and death. A balance between these two extremes must be achieved in which children are aware of life's dangers, understand the meaning and variable nature of risk, and recognize that they can enjoy the promise of all that life has to offer by exercising due care in pursuit of their goals.

How children view risk taking is governed by three basic concepts that influence children's perceptions of risk. They are (1) feeling in control, (2) familiarity, and (3) size of the event (Thygerson 1992).

Feeling in Control

Children who think they are in control of themselves and of the risk-taking experience will take more risks than those who perceive themselves to be lacking in control. Some children will thus subject themselves to the dangers of drugs, alcohol, tobacco, an unhealthy diet, sedentary lifestyle, or related high-risk behaviors because they feel comfortable and safe in participating in them. The sense of being in control is further enhanced if they or others apparently experience no adverse effects.

Familiarity

Children are more likely to expose themselves to danger (risk taking) in situations that are familiar to them, compared with situations with which familiarity is lacking. High-risk (dangerous) habits evolve out of repetitious practice and increased comfort despite ever-present dangers. Children are not likely to question the risk-taking nature of their behaviors when they feel comfortable, safe, and familiar.

Size of the Event

Highly visible situations or events in which property damage, injury, and death are widely publicized are feared more than equally dangerous situations receiving less attention. Consequently, riding in an automobile is thought by many to be less dangerous than air transportation. However, statistical data reveals just the opposite, indicating that automobile travel is more dangerous than air travel. Therefore, perceived safe, yet dangerous, activities are regularly practiced with little understanding or acceptance of the risks involved. Consequently, individual deaths and injuries arising from alcohol and tobacco use often go unnoticed, as do deaths and injuries arising from the misuse of firearms, unhealthy eating habits, lack of exercise, uncontrolled use of over-the-counter medications, and careless use of playground equipment.

Children who fail to understand the nature of their risk-taking behaviors are destined to become the victims of their own mismanagement. As children become more reality oriented in their understanding and management of risk, they will become caring human beings who exercise due care in all that they do.

Why Children Risk

Children take risks to satisfy their needs and wants. They often participate in risk taking ventures to:

- Save time
- Do things in a hurry
- Gain recognition and attention
- Meet a challenge or respond to a dare
- Protect themselves and others from danger
- Vent anger
- Attain things of value.

Children take short cuts involving their health, schoolwork, and chores to save time. They cross streets without looking, eat quickly, and fail to follow rules of safety because they are in a hurry to get things done. They may take drugs, tease other children, engage in vandalism, use humor, and speak out in support of others to gain recognition and attention. Still other children "hang out" with an older crowd, stay out late, and enjoy amusement-park rides because of the thrill and excitement they experience when doing things that require risk taking.

Children often do things on a dare that they would never consider doing on their own. They may likewise strive to meet challenges that set them apart from their peers, while other children may place themselves and others at risk in protecting themselves and their friends from danger. Children have died trying to save family members, friends, and pets from fire, drowning, and natural disasters. Some children are motivated to engage in high-risk behavior as a way of venting anger and frustration with situations not to their liking. Still other children are highly motivated to attain things of value. They will engage in risk-taking behavior to earn money, buy desired objects and instruments, and acquire status symbols that elevate their profiles in the groups to which they belong.

Risk Taking and Danger

For those who are aware of their options, risk taking is largely an act of choice. Unfortunately, many children are not always aware of their choices or the dangerous consequences. Children need assistance in weighing the potential gains of their actions and should cautiously examine the losses they are likely to experience. They must learn that not all risk taking is wise; they may be risking a lot for a little.

Risk taking in the absence of caring places the risk taker, others, and the environment in danger, and the consequences could be serious and irreversible. Children who are most likely to experience harm during risk-taking activities are "responders." Responder behaviors are triggered by environmental events. Frank calls Steve a name, and Steve responds in kind. Tony pushes Rob, and Rob pushes Tony. Responders act without thinking. All children are, by nature, responders in that they are biologically predisposed to react. They, like adults, are genetically hot-wired to respond even though they have the capacity to think, reason, and make sound decisions. The latter qualities, however, must be taught, while the former behavior is part of human nature.

Responders are already in the midst of danger when they act because they leave themselves no time to think. The urgency of the moment demands their quick attention and almost always places them in harm's way. Responders tend to commit fatal errors in judgment such as the following.

Error One

Not choosing an action because one does not know it is a possibility subjects risk takers to unreasonable danger. As an illustration, George is walking along a stream with his friend Mike. Neither boy can swim. George slips and falls into the water. Mike, a responder, quickly jumps into the stream to save his friend. Both boys drown. Mike's behavior is rather typical of a responder. He acted without thinking. His behavior was triggered by George's fall into the water. Mike had no time to think of other choices that would have lowered his and George's risk to danger while increasing the likelihood of a safe resolution to the situation for both boys.

Error Two

Choosing an action even though one does not know the possible outcome escalates the risk of danger. In the case of George and Mike, Mike never considered the fact that he might drown trying to save his friend, despite the odds against him. He never considered the fact that he could not swim and that he lacked instruction in water safety. Also, he never considered the fact that he was placing George's life in grave danger as well as his own.

Many children would not do the things they do if they stopped to consider the possible consequences of their actions. Children would not ride in motor vehicles without wearing their seat belts. They would not play with handguns and other dangerous weapons, and they would not swim alone or fail to wear protective headgear when riding their bicycles.

Error Three

Underestimating or overestimating the importance of information places children at high risk of experiencing danger. Mike overestimated his ability to save George from drowning, and he overestimated his skills and what he could offer his friend. George and Mike likewise underestimated the warning signs available to them. Their inability to swim, the rushing water, and the steep and crumbling bank were all warning signs that they did not heed. Mike underestimated the determination and strength of a drowning person trying to save his own life. He underestimated the speed of the current and the impact of the cold water on his body.

Children routinely underestimate the warnings of their parents, classroom and school safety rules, and societal laws. They underestimate the disabling and dangerous effects of illicit drugs and alcohol on their bodies and the impact of unhealthy eating habits, sleepless nights, and a sedentary lifestyle on their health and general well-being.

Children likewise overestimate the value of vitamins as a substitute for good nutrition, the medical community and its ability to correct the damage of unhealthy living practices, and the use of steroids to build strong bodies and boost self-esteem. Also, they overestimate the importance of buying designer clothing, smoking cigarettes, and "hanging out" with older peers as a way of being accepted and gaining social status.

Underestimating and overestimating the importance of life-determining information is likely to occur in the absence of reality testing. This practice is tantamount to high-stakes gambling, where the probability for loss far outweighs the likelihood of success.

Error Four

Relying on myths or assumptions as a basis for action increases children's exposure to danger. Myths and assumptions are not grounded in reality. They lack evidence to support their claims. Mike assumed that he would be able to save his friend by jumping into the water despite the fact that evidence was lacking to support his belief.

Some children operate under the myth that everyone should like them, while other children assume that all adults are kind, caring, and compassionate. Children, acting as responders, rarely question what they observe and are told. They rely on unsubstantiated beliefs and appearances as their tests for reality. Consequently, many children are easily taken in by other children and adults who manipulate the truth to gain compliance and power.

In other instances, children have been killed by guns that they assumed were not loaded; have been injured in car crashes driven by friends who were drinking but who appeared to be sober; and have taken drugs to get "high" believing (myth) that the drugs were perfectly safe to consume. Children who make type-four errors do so because they fail to test the credibility and accuracy of their own beliefs or the validity of what they have observed and have been told.

Managing Risk

While all life situations expose children to danger, danger itself is a variable condition that can be managed. Children have five strategies at their disposal that can help them to reduce the level of danger to which they are exposed when participating in any life situation. These strategies are:

- Risk avoidance
- Risk prevention
- Risk reduction
- Risk protection
- Risk acceptance.

Risk Avoidance

When the potential for experiencing personal harm is perceived to be high, children have the option of walking away from or otherwise avoiding danger to themselves, others, or the environment. The decision to avoid danger and thus lower one's personal exposure to harm is a personal choice and is affected by such variables as a child's perception of control of the situation, familiarity with the risk-taking experience, and the size or magnitude of the event itself. When children feel in control of what is happening, are familiar with the life situation through past exposure, and are not overwhelmed by the experience, they are more likely to accept risks rather than avoid them. The opposite is likely to be true when children experience fear or uncertainty because they do not feel in control of what is happening, lack familiarity with the experience, or are overwhelmed by the perceived size or intensity of the experience.

Knowledge is also a variable that impacts how children respond to risk. When children lack knowledge and make no attempt to secure it, they are likely to engage in involuntary high-stakes risk taking. Children who possess knowledge regarding the risks associated with a particular life experience or event have the option of using or ignoring the information when deciding what to do.

Billy, a sixth-grader, said "no" to a cigarette offered on the playground. He had learned about the dangers associated with smoking and did not want to subject himself to the harm that smoking cigarettes could do to his health. The strategy of risk avoidance seemed to him the right thing to do. Unfortunately, too many young people smoke because they ignore the warnings, feel in control of their own destiny, are familiar with others who smoke, and accept the practice because cigarette smoking does not appear to be as dangerous as others have made it out to be.

Risk avoidance is a useful strategy to consider when the potential for experiencing danger is high and the gains are minimal. Thygerson (1992), in discussing the relative nature of danger, offers the following guidelines to consider when judging whether or not to avoid a risk-taking situation:

- Never risk more than you can afford to lose
- Do not risk a lot for a little
- Consider the odds and your intuition.

Using these guidelines, children will find life situations like the following as ones to be avoided, because they pose significant harmful risks to those who participate in them:

- Swimming alone
- Riding in an automobile without wearing a seat safety belt
- Smoking tobacco products
- Eating a diet high in fat and low in vegetables and fruit.

Risk Prevention

Risk prevention represents those steps that children can take to lower their exposure to danger prior to participating in a risk-taking life situation. Riding a bicycle is a risk-taking experience with many potential dangers. However, some of these dangers can be eliminated or at least lowered with some careful preparation. Physical injury and possible death are the greatest risks. These risks often occur when bicycles are not kept in good repair, old and worn tires are not replaced, and brakes do not work properly. Danger also escalates when children do not have safe places to ride their bikes and lack basic knowledge of bicycle safety and the use of proper hand signals. Head and bodily injuries are most prevalent when children fail to wear protective clothing, such as a properly fitting bicycle helmet.

Much information is available regarding bicycle riding dangers and safety precautions that can be taken to reduce the risk of injury and increase bicycle safety. The literature is full of risk-prevention tips that can be implemented before Susan ever gets on her bicycle. Susan can lower her risk of danger by ensuring that her bicycle is mechanically safe to ride, that she has a safe place to ride it, that she possesses bicycle safety knowledge, and that she has the protective clothing and headgear needed for a fun and safe riding experience.

Risk prevention is a great strategy to use when anticipating potential dangers in the seven centers of care and identifying ways to manage these dangers before they can cause harm to self, others, or the environment. Risk prevention is a proactive strategy that all children can practice in response to all life situations. Risk prevention has practical application in food preparation, taking hikes in the woods, developing positive social relationships, health care, exercising, playing with friends, maintaining home safety, and using objects and instruments. Regardless of the life experience, there is much that children can do to care and be careful in their use of risk-prevention strategies.

Risk Reduction

While risk-prevention measures are applied in advance of a life situation, risk-reduction strategies are practiced during the experience itself. Children are encouraged to monitor carefully themselves, others, and the environment as they participate in what they are doing. Using their five senses, they are to be ever mindful of their actions and the steps they can take to reduce risks as they surface, before they can pose a threat to themselves, others, or the environment.

When children eat, they are told to chew their food carefully, refrain from talking while eating, and eat slowly. Following these risk-reduction guidelines, they can enjoy their food and reduce the risk of choking. When playing in a group, children are taught to use interpersonal risk-reduction skills as a means of promoting positive and responsible relationships. Following rules like speaking one at a time, maintaining eye contact, sharing, taking turns, and paying attention to what people are saying, doing, and feeling are all ways of enhancing interpersonal connections. Also, teaching children to recognize such warning signs as raised voices, angry words, and tense muscles can help them intervene by using learned social skills and other risk-management strategies to head off danger before it escalates into conflict. Reflection of feelings, deep breathing, goal setting and decision making, negotiating, anger management, peacemaking, and conflict resolution are all effective risk-reduction strategies that can be used as the need arises.

All life situations can be made safer when children practice risk-reduction strategies. When exercising, children can be taught to listen to their bodies as a way of gauging the intensity of their workout. Children can be taught to recognize muscle tension and relaxation and use risk-reduction measures to lower physical (body) and mental stress. Also, they can use time management, study skills, and organizational strategies to reduce the risk of not completing class assignments in a timely manner. Our goal as educators must be one of teaching children how learning risk-reduction strategies can help them to care for themselves, others, and the environment in the context of being careful.

Risk Protection

Risk-protection strategies relate to practices that children can use to protect themselves physically and emotionally from harm. For example, wearing sunscreen, shaded lenses, and protective clothing will help to shield children's bodies from overexposure to the sun's rays. Lifesaving vests worn while swimming and water-skiing provide buoyancy and offer protection from drowning. Automobile seat belts, bicycle helmets, and noise-level ear-protection aids are additional examples of risk-protection devices that reduce children's exposure to danger. Other examples of risk-protection strategies come in the form of healthy diets, exercise, the use of vitamins, inoculations, and medications that protect against what would be certain danger were they not used.

Risk-protection measures are also addressed in the design of toys with which children play, the bicycles they ride, and in the clothing they wear. Risk-protection agencies, local and national, strive to improve product safety and recall products that pose a danger to children's welfare. Risk protection is at the center of attention in the transportation industry, building and bridge design, road construction, and in the development of new medical breakthroughs. It is likewise present in environmental, plant, and animal protection policies designed to protect the earth's delicately balanced ecosystem.

We also teach children risk-protection strategies that enable them to care for their emotional and social selves. Positive thinking, rational thinking, self-affirmations, assertiveness training, goal setting, decision making, perspective taking, emotional management, conflict management, sharing, taking turns, listening to others, and so on provide children with the emotional and social strategies to protect themselves and enhance their relationships with others. Using these strategies, children are better prepared to give and receive care in the context of being careful (risk management).

Risk Acceptance

Children have the choice of either accepting or avoiding risk. Knowledge about risk therefore plays heavily into the equation of deciding what to do. Thygerson (1992) provided a useful four-statement continuum that has been adapted to help children consider what they know and do not know about the risks associated with their future actions.

1. I know and understand the risks.
2. I do not know about the risks (Risk is hidden).
3. Risk information is available, but I have not sought to attain it.
4. Risk is uncertain, or unknown, and no information is available.

For children to engage in true risk acceptance they must understand the dangers and the steps they can take to lower their exposure to harm (risk prevention, risk reduction, risk protection, risk avoidance, risk acceptance). After carefully considering the risks, the likelihood of their occurrence, and the degree to which they can be managed, the risk taker will be required to make a judgment call using Thygerson's (1992) three-test statements presented on pg. 163. Then and only then can children make a responsible and careful decision regarding whether or not to accept the risks that are unknown and those that cannot be managed.

Unfortunately, far too many children engage in risk-taking behaviors without understanding the risks. Encourage children to assess the risks known to them and seek additional available information before deciding what to do. If the risk is hidden, uncertain, or undefined, children may be risking more than they can afford to lose. The statistics are clear regarding the very high occurrence of unintentional injuries and death among children during their formative years. Perhaps some of these injuries and deaths could have been averted had children known more about the risks to which they were subjecting themselves.

Decision Making Lowers Risk

Children who live their lives as responders are far more likely to experience harm (physical and emotional) than those who function as decision makers. Responders are already in danger when their behavior is triggered by environmental stimuli. These children inevitably commit the four common errors of responders, thus opening themselves to danger. They fail to use environmental data to help them make caring and careful decisions.

Decision making is the single most important process that children can learn in becoming successful risk managers. Decision making helps children to avoid the four errors made by responders and teaches them how to:

- Increase their awareness of risk
- Measure risk to themselves, others, and the environment
- Judge the level of risk that they are willing to accept.

Awareness of Risk

Children learn to become more effective risk managers when they recognize that all life situations and actions carry a degree of risk. By improving their observational scanning skills and relying on available risk assessment information, children will increase their awareness of risk.

In addition to environmental risk factors are human risk factors that also increase children's exposure to danger (self, others, and environment) if not recognized and addressed. Some of these human factors are:

- Emotional (stress, personality factors, anxiety, depression, fear)
- Physical (illness, fatigue, impaired hearing, and sight)
- Cognitive (lack of knowledge and skills about self, others, and the environment)
- Personal (attitudes, values, thoughts, beliefs)
- Social (interpersonal, conflict, family issues)
- Medical (diseases, neurological, chemical abuse).

While only a partial list, these factors play heavily in the choices children make and the risks they take. Awareness of risk is greatly hampered when human risk factors cause other risk factors to go unnoticed. Risk factors that go unnoticed cannot be addressed and often surface when least expected, thereby compromising the safety of all who are affected by the choices being made.

Measure Risk

As children become aware of potential risk factors associated with a particular life situation, they will need to seek out all available information describing the risks and the likelihood of their occurrence. Children must learn to seek out reliable and valid data that will help them to understand the danger and probable impacts on people and property. Today, more than ever before, risk-management information is available on a variety of topics and life situations.

While scientific research data cannot tell who, when, or what may happen to a particular individual, it can provide useful group data regarding risk factors, rates of occurrence, the nature of harm, as well as predictive data projecting future harm to specific populations. Today children are able to access useful information pertaining to the risk factors associated with heart disease, high blood pressure, diabetes, and obesity. Risk factors are known for each of these conditions, as are the data measuring the risks to those who are already in danger. Preventative strategies are likewise known, and guidelines are available to follow in practicing a healthy lifestyle.

Risk-management data is available regarding cigarette smoking and health dangers, bicycle helmet usage and safety, medical treatment strategies and the risks for each, preventative health care measures and risk management, and early detection and survival strategies for life-threatening illnesses—all of which help people to make better decisions regarding the choices that are open to them. As children study the seven centers of care, they will be surprised by the amount of research data that is available regarding the risk factors that influence their choices as they seek to care in the context of being careful.

Children should be encouraged to conduct their own research in areas where data may be nonexistent. For example, children can research a life situation that involves crossing a street where the only control device is a stop sign. The biggest danger is getting hit by a car. Children can study this intersection by counting the number of cars that pass through it in a fifteen-minute period. The goal is to count the number of motor vehicles that come to a complete stop compared with those that slow down but do not stop. Children are now able to calculate how many cars used the intersection during the fifteen minutes and what percentages of them stopped and did not. From this observational data, children can state what the data implies and draw their own conclusions as to what they can do to reduce danger to themselves and others when crossing at this intersection.

Judge Risk

While measuring risk is scientifically based, judging whether or not to accept risk is a personal decision. Knowing the risk factors and the likelihood of their occurrence still leaves children with the responsibility of deciding for themselves how much risk they are willing to accept. The following three guidelines presented earlier in this chapter can help children to make the right choice for them (Thygerson, 1992).

Never Risk More than You Can Afford to Lose. With every life situation, there are risks and possible losses. Some losses can be permanent, while others may be difficult to recover from. If the potential for loss is thought to be high and the loss itself is likely to be great (significant), children may be risking more than they can afford to lose. The loss of a hard-earned reputation, a close friendship, or health can compromise a child's well-being and should therefore be weighed cautiously before any action is taken. Some difficult choices that children have faced in the past are the following:

- Whether or not to copy from a classmate's exam
- Whether or not to lie to a close friend
- Whether or not to keep or return money to a cashier who provided too much change.

Do Not Risk a Lot for a Little. If the gain is small and the danger is high, children may be risking a lot for a little. Children may feel compelled to do something on a dare or accept a challenge that could place them in danger. Bob is dared by his peer group to take something from a local grocery store without paying. Susan will receive fifty cents if she walks across the frozen pond near a sign that says, "Keep Off the Ice."

In addition to challenges and dares, anger and conflict are compelling emotions that sometimes get the best of people. Children are more likely to act out in ill-advised and dangerous ways when their emotions get the best of them. Bullying, acts of violence, and harm to people and property have occurred under such circumstances. Children are thus challenged to ask three questions before acting:

1. What do I stand to gain?
2. What do I stand to lose?
3. Is this something that I really want to do?

Consider the Odds and Your Intuition. Risk taking should not be taken lightly. The goal of risk taking is to grow from the experience, enjoy the gain, and most importantly, survive the risk (danger). Effective risk mangers seek to put the odds in their favor before acting (risk prevention, risk reduction, risk protection, risk avoidance, risk acceptance). They rely on different strategies and their "gut feelings" as useful sources of information and feedback. If children are uneasy or hesitant about their situation, they should listen to their heart, emotions (feelings), head (thoughts), and bodies (physical feelings) to decide what course of action to take.

Figure 5.1 illustrates a simple and easy-to-use decision-making model that emphasizes risk awareness, risk assessment, and risk judgment in helping children to become effective risk managers. "Stop, Think, & Go" decision making functions similar to a traffic signal light in that it helps children to exercise due care and caution at life's intersections when they must choose safe paths of travel in achieving their destination (O'Rourke & Worzbyt 1996; Worzbyt 1991; Worzbyt, O'Rourke, & Dandeneau 2003).

The traffic signal light model shown in figure 5.1 first instructs children to *Stop* and describe the life situation before them and then to state the goal they wish to attain. The goal is always stated in terms of caring and safety. For example, the life situation could be as simple as moving from the classroom to the cafeteria. The goal for this life situation would be to "Go from the classroom to the cafeteria in a caring and safe manner."

Next, children are instructed to proceed, with caution, to the *Think* stage of the model, where they are asked to identify (awareness) the risk factors associated with attaining their goal (going to the cafeteria). Some risk factors (dangers) are bumping into others in line; running into other hallway users; and tripping, slipping, and falling. Following the identification of risk factors, children are asked to assess the likelihood that these risk factors present a real danger to themselves and others. One way of doing this is to ask people in school (nurse, teachers, principal) if children have been injured in hallway accidents. Children also can discuss possible scenarios where the named dangers could occur. Lastly, children are asked to list things they can do to reduce or eliminate the dangers that have been identified.

In addressing the mentioned dangers, children are asked to consider risk-prevention, risk-reduction, and risk-protection strategies they can use. These strategies are then written as caring choices to be considered for implementation. Some examples of choices that children might consider are the following:

- Walk down the hallway
- Walk on the right side of the hallway

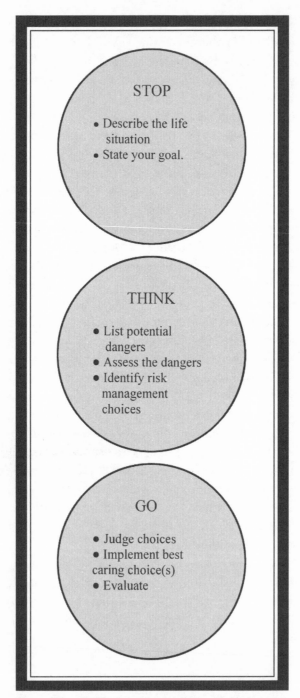

Figure 5.1.   Traffic signal light decision-making model.

- Maintain one arm's distance behind the person in front of you
- Make sure that your shoes are tied
- Watch for wet or slippery spots on the floor.

The last step in the process requires children to review the risk factors and the choices selected to reduce or eliminate them. Children may combine choices or select multiple choices that can be implemented in proper sequence. After careful consideration of their options (judging their safety) they are to *Go* with a plan that will help them to reach their goal in a caring and safe manner. The children in this case scenario decided to combine strategies and walk down the right side of the hallway at arm's distance from each other. They also decided to make sure their shoelaces are tied and to watch for and avoid wet or slippery spots on the floor.

In processing future risk-management decisions, refer to handout 5.1, which corresponds to the traffic signal light illustration in figure 5.1. This worksheet outlines the process presented on the preceding pages and will assist children in making thoughtful risk-management decisions.

Managing Risk in the Seven Centers of Care

Teaching children to care in the context of being careful is the right thing to do. Adults have the responsibility of helping children to understand that caring is not without risk and that they expose themselves to varying degrees of danger (risk) in everything they do. Consequently, we must teach our children how they can live full, complete, and happy lives by learning to care and to be careful in a world that can never be completely safe.

In this chapter, children will learn about the nature of risk, what it means to be a responsible and caring risk taker, and how to use risk-taking strategies in an effective decision-making model that will help them to choose wisely in support of themselves, others, and the environment. In the paragraphs that follow, the seven centers of care will once again be revisited. This time, we will explore some of the risks associated with caring in each center as well as review case studies that demonstrate how the five risk-management strategies (risk prevention,

STOP, THINK, & GO DECISION-MAKING WORKSHEET

Stop

1. Describe your life situation. _____

_____

2. State your goal (caring and safety). _____

_____

Think

3. List the potential dangers (risk factors). _____

_____

4. How do you know that these dangers are real (evidence)? _____

_____

5. Identify choices that can reduce or eliminate these dangers (risk prevention, risk reduction, risk protection, risk avoidance, risk acceptance):

• _____

• _____

• _____

• _____

Go

6. Review the dangers and your choices to lower your risk to danger. Judge for yourself the best plan of action to take. _____

_____

7. Implement and evaluate the success of your plan.

Handout 5.1

risk reduction, risk protection, risk avoidance, and risk acceptance) can be used in conjunction with Stop, Think, & Go decision making to help children care and to be careful.

Caring for Self

Throughout life, children strive to care for themselves. While all children are motivated to meet their needs and wants in a safe manner, they may not do so in the context of being careful. Regardless of the actions that children take, they believe they are making caring choices that will benefit themselves in some way. Consequently, behaviors such as smoking, drinking alcohol, fighting, lying, skipping school, cheating, being verbally abusive, chronic complaining, swearing, and teasing, often are children's best attempts at caring for themselves given the situations in which they find themselves. These behaviors, however, place children at greater risk of experiencing interpersonal conflict, pain, anger, fear, frustration, depression, physical and emotional stress, and lowered self-esteem.

When children fail to care for themselves in the context of being careful, they set themselves up for experiencing harm, harming others, and destroying property. Children must therefore be taught how to care for themselves while exercising due care. We want children to recognize that within all life situations are goals to be achieved, problems to be solved, and choices to be made that will help them to care for themselves in a safe manner.

In the following case study, Tom wants to receive a grade of B or better on his next math test, which is in one month. His goal is to obtain a grade of B or better in a caring and safe manner. As he contemplates his goal, he identifies the dangers that could keep him from succeeding. He listed dangers, like the following, that resulted in his obtaining a C on the last exam: not setting aside daily study time, failure to complete homework assignments, not asking for help when needed, and experiencing anxiety that comes from a lack of preparation and confidence. Given these risk factors, Tom brainstormed things that he could do to lower his risk of receiving a poor grade on his next math exam.

Tom thought of various risk-management strategies that he could use to counter the dangers he had identified. In the area of risk prevention, he decided to set aside one hour an evening to do his homework assignments and study. In the area of risk reduction, he decided he would ask

questions and receive the help he needed rather than waiting. With regard to risk protection, Tom decided to eat healthy meals, get enough
rest, and practice positive self-statements to build up his confidence.

Tom reviewed his choices in light of the dangers he had identified and
judged his plan to be workable in lowering his risk of receiving a low
grade while making caring choices that would help him to succeed. Tom
decided to *Go* with all of the choices he listed under the *Think* step of
decision making.

Caring for Intimate Others

Caring for family and friends is a worthy goal for all children to attain.
Caring involves helping others, respecting their privacy, taking turns,
sharing, listening to others openly, giving compliments, and graciously
accepting the care of others when needed.

Despite all that we know about caring for intimate others, doing so is
not without risk. Children, in their eagerness to help their friends, may
provide too much help and do for their friends what their friends must
learn to do for themselves. Some children lie, cheat, or steal to gain the
acceptance of their peer group. Other risk factors include taking others
for granted; criticizing family and friends; interrupting others; failure to
respond to others' feelings; being disagreeable; dealing with conflict in
a hostile, defiant, and aggressive manner; and abusing others with words
and actions. These risk factors endanger children's relationships with
others and can escalate into violence, hostility, anger, isolation, alien-
ation, loneliness, and the continuation of unhealthy social practices that
will negatively impact subsequent relationships.

Risk-management practices can go a long way in helping children to
examine their social goals and how best to achieve them in caring and
safety. Using Stop, Think, & Go decision making, Nancy wishes to offer
help to Martha, who seems to be having difficulty completing a creative
writing assignment. Her goal is to care for herself and Martha in offering
assistance to her. Nancy next considers the dangers and specific risks associated with offering help to someone who has not asked for it. She
identified the following risk factors. Martha might get angry and reject
her offer of help. Martha might want Nancy to do the assignment for her.
Martha might demand more time of Nancy than what Nancy has to give.

Nancy assessed the risks that she had written down. She knew Martha and had never known her to become angry with others. However, she did not have any information to help her assess the other risk factors. Given her understanding of what she would like to do (offer help to Martha) and the reality of the risks involved, Nancy identified actions she could take that would minimize her risks while caring for herself and Martha.

Nancy's plan is to approach Martha and say, "I was wondering if you would like some help with the writing assignment. I have about thirty minutes that I could spend with you if you would like some assistance." Nancy decided to use the open invitation as this would give Martha a chance to either accept or decline the help. If Martha accepts the help, Nancy will ask her how she can be of assistance being careful to let Martha do the work while she provides the support Martha needs. In this way she can care for Martha by allowing her to achieve success with minimal assistance.

Caring for Acquaintances and Distant Others

The dangers associated with caring for acquaintances and distant others are ever present. The most common risks relate to issues of discrimination and prejudice. Because people differ in age, racial and ethnic heritage, socioeconomic class, and sexual orientation, discriminatory practices often emerge among people of diversity. When this happens, the resulting effect is disrespect, unfair treatment, hidden anger, exclusionary practices, conflict, and victims of violence, crime, and hate.

Trusting and unsuspecting children are often the victims of those who disguise their intentions and lure the innocent into their traps of deception and mistreatment. Children have been abducted from shopping malls and their homes, and adults have fallen victim to those who prey on the elderly, sick, and infirm.

Despite the risks associated with caring for acquaintances and distant others, children must not withdraw from their caring and community-building mission in which they strive to support and enhance cooperation and inclusion among people of diversity. Only when the human race works together to build a caring and global community will we be able to create a circle of care in fighting poverty, reducing world hunger and conflict, curtailing worldwide illnesses, challenging life's inequities, and standing up to the "isms" that threaten cooperation and inclusion.

The utilization of risk-management strategies has much to offer children in their interactions with acquaintances and distant others. Martin, a sixth-grade student, is an eyewitness to the teasing of a third-grade girl (Beth) by a small group of children on the playground. They were taunting her because she is different from her peers. She is wearing old and tattered clothes. Her hair is dirty and not combed, and she is generally lacking in good hygiene.

Martin is shocked by the mean-spirited teasing he is witnessing and wants to help Beth. Using Stop, Think, & Go decision making, he reviews for himself what he is observing. Next, he formulates his goal, which is to care for Beth, himself, and the teasing youngsters in a safe and caring manner. Martin *Thinks* about the risks involved in caring for Beth. If the teasing continues, Beth will experience loneliness, isolation, and exclusion from her peers. Her self-esteem will be negatively affected, and she could experience physical injury if the teasing becomes too intense.

Martin also considers potential risks to himself and to the group of children doing the teasing. Depending upon what he says or how he handles the situation, he could negatively influence the dignity and self-respect of the children, who, feeling criticized, might take their frustrations out on him and Beth.

Having identified the risks, Martin assesses the possibility of their occurrence. He knows most of the children and thinks that they are basically good kids who are not intentionally seeking to hurt Beth. Nevertheless, the risks are real and have to be addressed.

Based on the known risks and his assessment of the situation, Martin begins to think of choices that would either eliminate or reduce the risks to himself, Beth, and those doing the teasing. Martin thought of risk-prevention, risk-reduction, and risk-protection strategies that he could use. He decided that one of his options was to approach Beth, give her a smile, and then face her teasers. At that moment, he would say, "I want you to stop teasing Beth. I know that you are all really good kids and would not want to hurt anyone. However, Beth is hurting right now and she needs our care and kindness."

Martin's strategy is to befriend Beth, stop the teasing, let the children know what Beth is feeling and what she needs, and to treat the teasers in a caring and respectful manner. Prior to *Going* with this choice, Martin judges the strategy to be safe and caring and decides to accept the risks in implementing his risk-management plan.

Caring for Nonhuman Animals

Caring for pets, domestic animals, and animals of the wild is not without risk to children and to the animals themselves. Children are always in danger of being harmed or killed if they are not careful in their treatment of animals. Animals also face danger when they experience cruel and inhumane treatment by people.

If children are to live in a climate of caring and safety in their relationship with animals, they must likewise be aware of and understand the dangers associated with animal contact and be prepared to manage the risks to which they are exposed. When children learn to care in the context of being careful in their treatment of animals, both children and animals will benefit from the caring relationships that emerge.

Morgan, who is six years old, loves animals. One Sunday afternoon she and her parents decide to visit the zoo. Prior to their visit, Morgan's parents review Stop, Think, & Go decision making with Morgan regarding how she can have a fun day at the zoo in a climate of caring and safety.

Morgan and her parents discuss their plans to visit the zoo and their goal, which is to have a caring and safe experience. In the context of achieving this goal, the family discusses some of the dangers present at the zoo and how those dangers can be lowered, thereby reducing their risk of harm.

Some of the dangers that the family discussed were getting lost or separated from each other, not reading and obeying zoo rules, getting too close to the cages, and feeding animals that were not to be fed by visitors. Having listed the dangers, Morgan's parents helped her to assess them and the likelihood of harm coming to those who ignored these dangers. They provided her with information from zoo publications and newspaper articles that told stories about people who were hurt by animals because they did not follow the rules and about how zoo animals are endangered by people who throw harmful objects and food into the cages.

Having reviewed the dangers, Morgan's parents tell her that they can have a safe and caring experience at the zoo by doing things that will lower their exposure to danger (risk). Here are a few of the strategies (choices) they listed.

- Morgan will walk hand in hand with her parents. Should she get separated from them, she will go to a zoo police officer and ask to be taken to the zoo visitors center, where her parents will meet her.
- Morgan and her family will stay on the zoo paths and behind the fences that surround the cages.
- Morgan and her family will read all zoo warning signs and follow their directions.

Morgan and her parents review their strategies and judge them to be useful in lowering their risk to danger. Pleased with their risk-management plan, they prepare for a safe and caring trip to the zoo.

Caring for Plants and the Physical Environment

Plants and the physical environment present their own set of risks. People are exposed to danger when they fail to exercise due care when interacting with plants and the environment. Likewise, plants and the environment are in danger when they are mistreated by people. Thus plants and the environment and people are dependent upon each other for their care and safety. Neither can survive without the other's caring actions.

Nancy (ten years old) enjoys the woods and the serenity of long peaceful hikes. The woods provide comfort, relaxation, and solitude. The natural beauty is breathtaking and is music to the senses.

In years past, Nancy has hiked with family members, but would now like to take a five-mile hike in the woods with a close school friend. Her goal is to complete the hike in a way that is caring and safe for herself and her friend Jill.

Using the Stop, Think, & Go decision-making model she learned at school, she begins to consider her goal and what she must do to achieve a safe and caring outcome. The process begins with a review of what Nancy and Jill want to do, which is to take a caring and safe five-mile hike.

Next, Nancy and Jill consider the risks that such an adventure might present. Not sure what all the dangers might be, they visit a local hiking club and ask for literature on planning a safe hike. Some of the dangers they discovered that would need their attention were the following:

- Getting lost
- Failing to notify others of their hiking plans
- Falling and becoming injured
- Lacking sufficient food and water
- Facing a too-challenging hike that might exceed their ability
- Experiencing rapidly changing weather conditions
- Failing to dress appropriately.

Having identified these dangers, any one of which could subject Nancy and Jill to harm, they assessed their probability of occurrence. The hiking book indicated that these dangers were real and that thousands of hikers every year subject themselves to needless injury or death because they failed to apply appropriate and caring risk-management strategies.

Using the information they have, Nancy and Jill set out to identify strategies that will help them eliminate or reduce the risks and increase their care and safety. Using their list of potential dangers and their knowledge of risk-prevention, risk-reduction, and risk-protection strategies they set out to plan a low-risk hiking experience.

Some of the risk-prevention strategies they identified were locating novice hiking trails in their area, securing topographical maps of the hiking area, obtaining a first aid kit, and buying a compass, which they know how to use. In the area of risk protection, they decided to buy sturdy hiking boots, pack layers of clothing and rain gear, and take sufficient food and water for a one-day hiking trip. Risk-reduction strategies consisted of registering their hike at the local state police headquarters, checking weather conditions on the day of the hike, and walking slowly and apart from each other to ensure good footing.

As they reviewed the risks and their hiking strategies, they believed themselves to have a sound risk-management plan. To make sure they had not overlooked something important, they reviewed their plan with a hiking club member. Judging the plan to be fit for execution, Nancy and Jill decided to *Go* on their hike.

Caring for the Human-Made World of Objects and Instruments

Children live in a world of objects and instruments most of which were created to benefit themselves, others, and the environment. However, for every object and instrument that has been created to protect, entertain, and improve the quality of life, there are inherent dangers and varying degrees of risk to those who use them.

The dangers posed by objects and instruments tend to increase when they are misused or not properly maintained and stored, and when they fail to meet manufacturer's safety guidelines. Thus, lawn mowers, bicycles, pencils, space heaters, sports equipment, computers, smoke alarms, medicines, and clothing are examples of objects and instruments that have the potential either to help or harm. Children must therefore be taught how to become effective risk managers in the care of objects and instruments so that they may derive maximum benefit from their use in a climate of safety and caring.

Justin, eleven years old, wants to start mowing the family lawn so that he can earn an allowance. Justin's dad thinks he is old enough to take on the responsibility, but not without a lesson in risk management. Justin's dad takes him through the Stop, Think, & Go decision-making model. He tells Justin that his goal must be to mow the lawn in a caring and safe manner. He then explores with Justin the potential dangers of lawn mowing and requires Justin to read the mower's user manual.

The dangers that Justin and his dad list include injuries to eyes from flying objects, hearing loss from the running mower, and slips and falls that could bring him into contact with the rotating mower blade. He also learned about the dangers of filling the gasoline tank while the engine block is hot and of running the mower without maintaining the proper oil level.

The user's manual was clear in identifying and discussing the potential dangers of using a lawn mower. The only way a safe mowing experience can be assured is if the user's manual directions are followed exactly as printed. After reviewing the user guidelines, Justin now understands why they must be followed—to help ensure his safety. The guidelines specified the importance of wearing protective clothing and eye and ear protection devices. Guidelines were provided for proper maintenance, fueling, and mowing.

Justin understands the importance of following all the rules specified in the manual and judges his ability to care for himself and have a safe mowing experience as high. He decides that he has a sound risk-management plan to follow and is eager to begin mowing the family lawn.

Caring for Ideas

Ideas provide direction, offer protection, and stimulate creativity. Ideas shape children's beliefs, attitudes, and values. Ideas provide the moral compass that helps children to determine right from wrong. Ideas set the stage for action and give life purpose and meaning. Also, ideas help shape children's quality of life in a circle of care in which they learn how to become providers and receivers of care.

As important as ideas are in fostering a quality world, they have the potential for doing harm as well. Ideas that are based on myth, that distort reality, and are created for the purpose of taking advantage of others, manipulating the truth, or fostering exclusion and competition have the potential for destroying caring and community building.

False ideas evolve out of ignorance and fear. The AIDS epidemic was fueled by misinformation, a lack of understanding, and fear. Lies also are ideas that are designed to protect the guilty and the devious, instill prejudice and oppression, and take unfair advantage of people by manipulating the truth.

Children must be taught to examine the soundness of their ideas and those of others, the risks in receiving and sharing responsible and irresponsible ideas, and the risks associated with standing up for what is right and responsible in a world driven by ideas that have the potential for doing harm as well as good.

Christine, a seventh-grader, was the recipient of information (ideas) that came in the form of a Sunday morning infomercial on a piece of exercise equipment that would supposedly tone her stomach muscles and help her to lose up to five pounds per week. The people demonstrating the equipment had the "look" that she wanted for herself. Slightly overweight, Christine was impressed by the before-and-after photos of people who used the stomach exerciser and was especially impressed with the testimonials from "everyday people" who spoke highly of the equipment and how it had changed their lives in just twenty minutes a day, three days a week.

The infomercial instructed viewers to go to their phones "now" and order the stomach exerciser at a 20 percent discount and also receive a free video, dietary supplements, and a six-week eating plan guaranteed to reshape one's body in just six weeks or your money back, no questions asked.

Christine had some money and her own credit card. She immediately went to the phone and ordered the stomach exerciser, all of the additional gifts included. After receiving the equipment, Christine followed all of the instructions, but at the end of six weeks she was deeply disappointed in the results. She put the entire program aside, never to use it again.

Had Christine taken time to make a responsible decision using the Stop, Think, & Go decision-making model, she might not have wasted her time and money. Christine's goal was to tone her stomach and lose weight in a caring and safe manner. Buying anything without checking it out opens the buyer to a variety of inherent risks:

- Paying for something and never receiving it
- Obtaining a product that may or may not perform as advertised
- Receiving a product that could be harmful to one's health.

Had Christine thought of these risks, she could have discussed them and the exercise equipment with her parents, teachers, physician, and health and physical education instructor. They would have told her that these risks are real and should be addressed before purchasing the equipment. They probably would have suggested that she also consider other choices in helping her to achieve her goal in caring and safety.

Christine could have investigated the company through a variety of consumer advocacy groups, read unbiased reports on the equipment and the claims being made, and consulted with experts (nurse, doctor, health and physical education teacher) to obtain their feedback on the commercial's claims. Had she done all of these things, Christine might have judged the purchase to be too risky and avoided buying the equipment. She then could have pursued other choices that would have helped her achieve her goal.

ROLE OF FACILITATOR

Your goal is to help your children understand the nature of risk and risk taking. Risk relates to children's exposure to danger. Risk taking is what children do when they participate in life situations involving danger. You will want to help your children understand that all life situations expose them to some degree of danger, since nothing in life is completely safe. The good news is that while danger is a condition of life and living, it can be managed. Children can learn to lower their personal risk to danger so that it falls into an acceptable range of risk, or they can avoid situations where the risk to harm is too high.

Throughout the remainder of this chapter, your children will be participating in a variety of life experiences and activities that will help them to increase their awareness of risk, assess their exposure to it, and judge for themselves whether to accept or avoid the risk. Your children will be learning how to become effective risk managers using Stop, Think, & Go decision making and using five risk-management strategies that will help them to give and receive care in the context of being careful. You will be teaching your children how to enjoy life to the fullest in a climate of caring and safety.

Have fun teaching your children how to care and to be careful using what they have learned about risk management. Help them to understand how they can become givers and receivers of care in the seven centers of care while successfully managing the risks that are inherent in caring.

BENEFITS TO CHILDREN

Children who are responsible and effective risk managers:

- Understand the meaning of risk and risk taking
- View caring and being careful from a decision-making perspective
- Manage dangers using five risk-management strategies
- Make caring and careful choices in the seven centers of care
- Enjoy life and living in a climate of caring and safety.

PITFALLS TO CHILDREN

Children who are high risk takers and poor risk managers:

- Participate in daily life situations without considering the dangers or personal risks to themselves
- Experience a high rate of unintentional injury, death, and property damage
- Expose others and the environment to unacceptable dangers
- Act without considering the consequences of their actions
- Fail to challenge the accuracy of the information that influences their behavior.

ACTIVITIES

What's My Risk?

Objectives

1. To help children understand the nature of risk
2. To help children identify situations and events involving risk
3. To help children understand that they can reduce risk to themselves.

Group Size: Classroom group or small work groups
Time: 15 to 30 minutes
Materials: Life situation index (three-by-five) cards
Facilitator: The purpose of this activity is to help children understand the nature of risk, identify situations involving risk, and explore ways in which they can lower risk to themselves, others, and the environment. Begin by explaining that risk refers to the degree or amount of danger to which someone is exposed. Risk is therefore a variable condition, in that no two people participating in the same life situation will be exposed to the same level of risk (danger).

To help your children understand risk, tell them that two children are riding bicycles. One is wearing a safety helmet, the other is not. Ask them if one child is at a higher risk of being injured than the other and why they believe this is true. Most of the children will tell you that the child not wearing the helmet is at greater risk of experiencing harm, because his head is not protected in the event of a fall.

Help your children understand that nearly every life situation or event in which they participate has an element of risk. Explain to your children that by being aware of the dangers, they can do things (act) to reduce risk to themselves, others, and the environment. Tell your children that they will be participating in some activities that will help them to understand the nature of risk and actions they can take to lower it.

Process

1. Present the following situation to your children. Lifting heavy objects is a danger to you because (let your children fill in the blank). One response that you are likely to get is that lifting a heavy object can cause a back injury. Ask your children to list some things that a person can do to reduce their risk of a back injury. Some answers your children might give you are: do not lift the object; ask for help in lifting it; use a pulley to lift it.

2. Now present your children with a number of life situations written on separate index cards. As each situation is presented, ask your children to identify a potential danger (harm) and one thing they can do to lower their risk to that danger.

Life Situation	Danger	Lower Risk
Walking on a road	Hit by a car	Wear reflective clothing
Riding in a motor vehicle		
Eating lunch		
Rushing through a math assignment		
Fighting on the playground		
Sitting in the sun		
(other ideas)		

Discussion

1. Ask your children to explain how they decide when something might place them at risk of being harmed. Answer: They think about the consequences of their actions before acting.

2. Help your children understand that they participate in many daily life situations. Each life situation presents dangers that can be reduced if they are aware of them. Ask your children to identify some of their daily life activities, the dangers they pose, and actions they can take to reduce them: crossing a street at an intersection, rocking back in a chair, brushing one's teeth, riding on the school bus, looking at someone else's paper, running in the hall, and playing on the playground.

3. Ask your children to read the newspaper, watch television news, read stories, watch movies, and observe life situations from the school bus window. Ask them to identify the helpful and hurtful choices they see people making that either lower their exposure to danger or increase it. Discuss these choices and how they raise or lower one's risk of being harmed.

Responding to Risk: What Can I Do?

Objective: To help children understand and practice five strategies they can use to safely reduce their daily exposure to danger.

Group Size: Classroom group or small work groups

Time: 30 minutes

Materials: (Optional) transparency of the five methods used to manage risk

Facilitator: Help your children to understand that taking risks is a part of life. However they can learn to take care of themselves, others, and property when they are exposed to possible dangers. Help them understand that in the preceding activity they became more aware of risk. In this activity, you will be teaching your children five methods they can use to lower their daily exposure to risk. These methods are designed to help children have fun and meet their goals in an environment of relative safety. Children in grades six through eight will be able to understand the five methods of risk management and will be able to provide good examples for each method. However, young children are likely to become confused and may have difficulty in understanding the differences and similarities among the various risk-management methods. Therefore when teaching risk-management strategies to younger children, place the emphasis on lowering risk and not on requiring children to provide correct responses for each method. Modify the activities that follow with respect to your children's development and their ability to grasp the concepts being taught.

Process

1. During the first half of this activity, you will be teaching your children five ways in which they can lower their risk to danger. Each method is defined and accompanied by an example. Following each example is a question to engage your children in further thought.

   Risk Avoidance: When a situation is so dangerous that the risk of injury, death, or property damage is high, a wise decision is to avoid participating in it. For example, Billy avoids bicycle riding when he does not have a bicycle helmet to wear. Ask your children to identify life situations they would avoid because the danger involved would place them or others at high risk (playing with fire).

   Risk Prevention: Actions that children can take to stop or lower their risk of danger to themselves, others, or the environment prior to participating in the risk-taking situation. For example, prior to taking a day hike in the woods, children decide to buy plastic bags so they can carry out their trash and not harm the environment. Ask your children what preventative measures they can take to ensure for a safe home, academic grades of B or higher, and good health.

   Risk Reduction: Actions that children can take to reduce the risk of danger to themselves, others, and the environment while participating in a risk-taking situation. For example, crossing a street even at a crosswalk can be dangerous. Children can reduce personal risk to themselves by looking both ways (left, right, and left again) before and *while* crossing the street. Swimming, bicycle

riding, hunting, riding in a car, and answering the door when someone knocks all have their dangers. Ask your children what they can
do to lower their risk of danger while doing these activities.

Risk Protection: Actions that children can take to care for
themselves physically and emotionally when participating in a risk-
taking situation. For example, children who wear teeth guards
when playing contact sports are protecting their teeth from being
injured. Ask your children to identify steps they can take to protect
themselves (physically or emotionally) from danger when riding in
a car, riding a bicycle, playing sports, walking along a dark road,
and maintaining a healthy body and mind.

Risk Acceptance: An action that children take when they have
fully explored a life situation or activity, have done what they can
to reduce the risk of harm, judge the danger to be low, and decide
to participate in the experience knowing that nothing is completely
safe. For example, riding a bicycle can be dangerous to the rider
and to others. However, if the rider understands the risks and man-
ages them effectively using the strategies discussed, a child may
deem bike riding to be relatively safe and accept the risks. Ask your
children to describe risk-taking activities in which they participate.
Help them understand that nothing is completely safe but that
they can lower their risk to danger using the risk-management
strategies they have been discussing. Select a few activities provided by your children and have them discuss how they can make
them safer using the five risk-management strategies.

2. Now present your children with a variety of life situations. Help
   your children understand how they can apply more than one strategy to the same life situation in controlling risk. For riding a bicycle:
   • Risk prevention: keep your bicycle in good repair
   • Risk reduction: ride at a speed in which you can control your
     bike
   • Risk protection: wear a bicycle helmet
   • Risk acceptance: do all you can to control known risks and ac-
     cept the fact that bike riding does involve some risk.
3. Risk-taking situations: What method(s) can you use to lower your
   risk in the following situations:

- Smoking cigarettes
- Asking questions in class
- Riding in a car
- Playing baseball
- Staying home alone
- Answering the door when home alone
- Walking along a roadway
- Hiking in the woods
- Staying healthy
- Receiving good grades
- Other: Select various activities from the seven centers of caring.

DISCUSSION

1. Help your children recognize that they have learned five strategies they can use to care and to be careful. Help them to set goals in which they can use one or more of these strategies in making caring choices in the seven centers of care.
2. Learning to be careful begins when children fully appreciate the nature of risk and respond to it in ways that enhance their safety and caring. Use newspaper articles, literature, movies, television programs, and the news to explore further the concepts of risk and risk management.
3. Identify ways in which people in a variety of occupations use the five risk-management strategies to increase caring and safety for themselves, others, and the environment.

Homework

1. Ask your children to create a variety of case study situations that will give them practice using the five risk-management strategies when making Stop, Think, & Go decisions.
2. Ask your children to identify real life situations in which risk-management strategies were used. Discuss three examples in class.

Susan's Dilemma

Objectives: To help children learn how to become effective risk managers using Stop, Think, & Go decision making.

Group Size: Individuals, small groups, or classroom group

Time: 15 to 30 minutes

Materials: Stop, Think, & Go decision-making worksheet (see handout 5.1, introduced earlier in the chapter) and the story "Susan's Dilemma"

Facilitator: The purpose of this activity is to help your children incorporate everything they have learned about risk management into a single and easy-to-use decision-making model. The model uses a traffic signal light to teach children a valuable three-step process that will help them to care for themselves, others, and the environment in the context of being careful (reducing their exposure to harm). The Stop, Think, & Go decision-making model teaches children to Stop and describe their life situation and state their goal with caring and safety in mind. Next, they are asked to Think about their situation in terms of identifying the potential dangers (risk factors) involved. Having done this, they are asked to consider each danger and the evidence they have that makes this danger real. Now, they are challenged to identify things they can do (choices) to lower or eliminate these dangers. In the Go stage of the model, children are to review the dangers for this life situation, the choices they have selected to reduce these dangers, and then judge for themselves which caring and safe choices will help them to meet their goal.

Process

1. Explain to your children that they will be learning how to make Stop, Think, & Go decisions.
2. Begin by showing children a picture of a traffic safety signal. Ask them what it is and how it is used by pedestrians and motor vehicle drivers to lower their risk of harm and increase their safety.
3. Now introduce the Stop, Think, & Go decision-making model. This can be done showing your children a drawing with three ver-

tical circles colored red, yellow, and green and in which the words "Stop," "Think," and "Go" are printed. Discuss the similarities between this drawing and the traffic safety signal light. Tell your children that Stop, Think, & Go decision making will help them to lower their risk to danger and increase their safety when they use it to help them make caring and safe choices.

4. Explain to your children that you are going to teach them how to make a Stop, Think, & Go decision by telling them a story entitled "Susan's Dilemma."

5. Read "Susan's Dilemma" (at the end of this section) and stop where it says to. Discuss the story with your children.

6. Give your children a copy of the Stop, Think, & Go decision-making worksheet (handout 5.1).

7. Now guide your children through the worksheet using "Susan's Dilemma."

8. First, ask your children to describe what is happening in the story. Answer: Tom asks Susan to leave the lifeguard supervised swim area and go with him to a place farther down the beach. Some of Susan's friends decide to go with Tom.

9. Have your children write a goal for Susan with caring and safety in mind. Answer: To enjoy swimming in caring and safety.

10. Susan is to *Think* of the dangers that could happen to her if she leaves the lifeguard-supervised area. Ask your children to brainstorm some possible dangers and write them down on the worksheet.

11. Ask your children to discuss whether they believe these dangers are real. Ask them to explain why they think these dangers may exist.

12. Now ask your children to list things that Susan can do to lower her risk to these dangers. They can use the risk-management strategies listed to guide them in their thinking.

13. Ask your children to review Susan's dilemma, the dangers involved, and the choices listed to reduce these dangers.

14. Ask your children to decide (judge) what they think Susan should do given her dilemma. There are many acceptable choices. There is no one right or correct response.

15. Now read the conclusion to this story and discuss the ending and how Stop, Think, & Go decision making might have helped Susan to "play it safe."

Discussion

1. Stop, Think, & Go decision making helps children to care for themselves, others, and the environment. Explain.
2. Discuss how Stop, Think, & Go decision making can be used in other life situations similar to those discussed in this chapter.

Susan's Dilemma

Susan is swimming at Cayuga Lake State Park with a group of her friends when Tom suggests they leave the lifeguard-supervised area and go to a place farther down the beach where they can be by themselves. Some of Susan's friends decide to go with Tom. What should Susan do?

Stop Here

Do not read beyond this point. Discuss Susan's dilemma using the Stop, Think, & Go decision-making worksheet (handout 5.1 on pg. 174). Refer to the process section of this activity for directions in guiding your children through the model.

The Rest of the Story

Some of Susan's friends stayed in the lifeguard-protected swim area, but Susan went with her friends, Tom, Jill, and Bob. They found a quiet place down the shoreline away from everyone else.

In the midst of their fun, Susan began to scream. "My leg is caught under the water! I can't move! Please, somebody help me!" Susan, in her panic to get loose, became more entangled in the grass and logs below. Tom and Bob tried desperately to free Susan, who was now having difficulty keeping her head above water.

Bob decided to run for help while Tom held Susan's head above water so she could breathe. Some thirty minutes later, Susan was freed by the local volunteer fire department rescue squad. Susan's big scare is something that she will never forget, and neither will her friends.

SUGGESTED ACTIVITIES FOR THE WEEK

Language Arts and Reading

Reading, writing, and speaking are all forms of communication that can be used to raise or lower children's exposure to danger. The goal in chapter 5 is to help children understand how they can use all forms of communication to lower their risk to harm and become effective risk managers. For example, explore with your children how they can use poetry, humor, and reading for pleasure to prevent or reduce their exposure to stress. Explain to them the value of being able to communicate effectively using appropriate (caring) interpersonal skills in managing risk (good manners, anger management, conflict resolution, listening, and speaking one at a time) in social situations.

Through reading, writing, and speaking, children can gain awareness and understanding regarding various forms of harm that threaten the seven centers of care. With this understanding, they can utilize a variety of risk-management strategies in caring for themselves, others, and the environment.

Explore with your children, using books, films, newspaper articles, and television programs, life situations that depict risk taking in the seven centers of care. Use the risk-management strategies discussed in chapter 5 to help your children become effective risk managers in which they identify, measure, and judge the risks depicted. Role play and discuss ways in which these dangers (harm) can be responsibly managed.

Math

Numbers play a significant role in children's lives in helping them to identify, measure, judge, and manage risk in favor of caring and safety. Numbers warn of danger. They help children to assess the magnitude of risk and assist them in monitoring the level of risk to which they, others, and the environment are exposed.

Explore with your children how people in various occupations use numbers to care and to be careful in protecting themselves and the people they serve. Help your children to understand how they can use numbers to make caring and safe decisions.

Work with your children to examine ways in which they can use numbers in their own lives to manage risk using some of the strategies in chapter 5. Children can be taught how to use numbers when making decisions regarding the intensity of their workouts, cooking meals, storing food, deciding what and how much to eat during the day, monitoring body signs that warn of danger (blood pressure, heart rate, body temperature, cholesterol levels, body weight, and so on), and understanding how numbers can be used to reduce danger when riding their bicycles (tire inflation and speed), playing sports (body warning signs), and swimming (monitoring water depth).

Help your children understand how numbers are used to reduce risk and increase safety in the seven centers of care. Give them an opportunity to explore, understand, and use numbers in ways that will help them to raise their awareness, measure, and judge the level of danger to which they, others, and the planet are exposed and actions they can take to help lower those dangers. Water tables, ozone levels, and animal populations need to be monitored and actions taken to maintain the balance of nature. Work with your children in identifying a variety of ways in which numbers can be used to measure, monitor, and reduce the dangers that threaten their safety.

Remind your children that numbers exist for one reason and one reason only—to help them care and be careful in managing risk in the seven centers of care. When you teach children about numbers and how to use them, do so in the context of helping them to understand how numbers are used to make wise and caring decisions.

Science

Science is the systematic study of all things in which people seek to gain awareness and new understandings of the physical world and the universe. Science is a caring discipline in which scientists seek to improve the quality of life for humankind and to monitor and maintain a favorable balance of nature in sustaining the circle of care in support of life and living as we know it.

Scientists investigate the mysteries of the unknown and the seemingly unexplainable. They seek to know more about the known and to offer new information and explanations regarding discoveries that will help people care more deeply, manage risk more responsibly, and live life more fully.

Help your children to explore ways in which the various sciences have contributed to new knowledge, procedures, equipment, and medical breakthroughs that have helped improve caring and safety in the seven centers of care. Explore the dangers to which scientists are exposed and steps they take to lower their risk to these dangers (risk management).

Help your children understand how scientific breakthroughs have both decreased and increased people's exposure to risk.

Explore with your children the fact that dangers are not always known and how scientists have lost their lives in pursuit of their dreams. Help children understand what motivates people to take the risks they do in trying to improve the lives of others. Discuss the dangers and risk-taking ventures of those people who participate in medical research and space exploration, and who explore the ocean depths in search of the unknown.

Science has contributed much to the quality of children's lives in helping them to become more effective in making caring decisions. Help your children to understand that they must use caring information, devices, and medical breakthroughs if they are to benefit from what others have provided. For example, we now know the causes of many diseases and steps that children can take to prevent or reduce the dangers to which they are exposed (obesity, cancer, heart disease, diabetes, sexually transmitted diseases, etc). Nonetheless, despite available risk-management information, many of these diseases are on the rise. Today, children's toys are safer, vehicular travel is less risky, and diagnostics procedures that screen for the early detection of diseases are more prevalent. Medications designed to prevent or slow down the progression of many diseases are also available, but they must be used if they are to derive the care for which they were designed.

Science has done much to improve the quality of children's lives through the use of risk-prevention, risk-reduction, risk-protection (inoculators), and risk-avoidance measures (don't smoke or abuse drugs, etc.). Help your children understand the caring nature of science and how they can use what they learn from science in the seven centers of care.

Social Studies

When people of diversity come together, either by choice or circumstance, the potential for danger (harm) is always present, as is the potential for caring hearts and hands. Social studies can help children understand group dynamics, why people join groups, dangers in groups, and the conflicts that sometimes arise within and between groups. The study of social interaction and group dynamics can help caring children strive to establish a common humanity and an interdependent global community supported by shared values and shared responsibilities.

While we still have a long way to go in fulfilling Dr. Martin Luther King's "I Have a Dream" speech, caring people the world over are making strides in declaring a universal declaration of human rights and making inroads against conflicts and social challenges that threaten our global community (diseases, poverty, racial unrest, terrorism, wars, illness, and so on).

Encourage your children to be social scientists and to learn steps they can take in caring and being careful in their relationships with people they know and don't know. Help them understand steps they can take in managing risk in relation to developing and maintaining a caring social discourse with others. They can learn to do this by developing effective social-interpersonal skills, understanding diversity in all its forms, learning perspective in examining other's view points, being sensitive to interpersonal signs of danger, and managing potential conflicts before they escalate into harm.

Teach your children how to disagree while remaining civil and respectful. Help them to live and appreciate the value of diversity and to "stand up" for what is right by doing what is right for all the right reasons. Help your children to become involved in social challenges in their community that threaten the lives of those in it. Children can play an active role in promoting the health and wellness of their community through social service.

Above all, help your children learn from historical and present-day global conflicts the dangers that exist when people of diversity fail to find common ground, shared values, and shared responsibility in establishing and maintaining a common humanity. Help your children *notice* when things are not as they should be (social injustices), find the *courage* to "stand up" for what is right, and *act* in the name of caring and basic goodness as a caring person and a builder of caring communities.

Health and Physical Education

Health and physical education classes are all about helping children care and to be careful. Our goal as teachers (caring adults) must be one of helping children develop a wellness lifestyle in which children learn how to care for themselves physically, mentally, and spiritually (living a life of meaning and purpose through caring).

Because children live in a global environment, their health and wellness is affected not only by the caring and careful choices they make in their own behalf but also by the caring and careful choices they make in the remaining six centers of care. The goal, when teaching children to care, is to help them understand that what they care for will influence the level of care which they enjoy. Thus children must be taught how caring for intimate others, distant others, plants and the environment, nonhuman animals, human-made objects and instruments, and ideas impacts the quality of their lives.

Children can reduce harm to themselves by using effective risk-management strategies with regard to the self-care choices they make. They can also reduce harm to themselves and increase their personal safety by caring and being careful regarding the choices they make in the remaining six centers of care.

Teach your children how to use the five risk-management strategies and Stop, Think, & Go decision making in making caring risk-management decisions regarding their health and wellness. Explore with them the life choices that they face daily and how what they are learning in their health and physical education classes will help them care and be careful. Provide them with hypothetical and real-life situations to ponder and resolve using caring strategies that will improve the quality of their lives. Help them see the relationships between what they are learning in the classroom and life applications, applications that they can use in caring for themselves, others, and the environment.

TIPS FOR CAREGIVERS

Helping children care and be careful suggests that caring is not without danger. Everything that we know about caring (giving and receiving care) suggests that there is always the potential for harm to oneself, others, and the environment. Given that danger is a condition of caring, one might think that withdrawing from life is the only way to stay safe. This action is also dangerous, in that children who choose to hide from danger experience it anyway—in lost relationships, lives of fear, and existences that are uneventful and boring, if not depressing. Despite all that children might do to avoid or escape danger, it is always present.

While danger is a part of life and living, the good news is that we can teach children to manage their exposure to it. Children need to understand that no two people are exposed to the same levels of danger when experiencing a life situation or event. Danger is a variable condition known as risk. While children can not completely eliminate danger from their lives in favor of safety, they can learn how to lower their risk (exposure) to danger. They can do this by becoming aware of its presence and then using risk-management ideas (strategies) to lower their exposure to it.

Your goal is to help your children understand what it means to give and receive care in the context of being careful. Help your children realize that they can care more deeply and live life more fully when they learn how to increase their awareness of danger, how to measure it accurately, and how to judge critically their exposure to it.

The suggestions, activities, and tips that follow will help you to help your children care and be careful using a variety of proven risk-management strategies that are designed to decrease risk and increase safety in all that children do.

1. Help your children understand the meaning of danger. Answer: Danger relates to children's personal exposure to harm.
2. Review with your children the presence of danger in the seven centers of care. Help them to understand that caring and danger are inseparable. Your goal is not to scare your children but merely to point out a simple reality of life.
3. Introduce your children to the word "risk." Use the word in a sentence and then ask them to define it for you. Answer: Risk refers to the degree or amount of harm (danger) to which children are exposed. Explain that no two people participating in the same life situation will be exposed to the same degree of personal danger. That is because people's exposure to danger will go up or down depending on the choices they make and the actions they take. For example, Tom and Judy are riding in the back seat of their parent's

car. Tom wears a seatbelt. Judy does not. Which child is at greater risk, and why?

4. To help your children better understand the nature of risk, present them with a number of life situations. Ask them to name one potential danger for each and one action they can take to lower their risk to danger.

Life Situation	Danger	Lower Risk
Eating	Choking	Take small bites and chew thoroughly
Exposure to sun	Sunburn	Wear sun screen
Hiking in woods		
Riding a bicycle		
Staying home from school		

5. Help your children understand that every life situation presents some level of danger from feeding an animal to crossing a street. Explain to them that their risk to harm goes down when they make caring choices that reduce their exposure to danger.

6. Ask your children to name some daily life situations and activities in which they participate. For each item they list, ask them to identify one danger to themselves, others, or the environment and one choice they can make to lower their risk to harm.
   • Playing baseball, feeding a pet, packing a lunch
   • Crossing streets, mowing the lawn, staying up late
   • Going to the mall, walking in the hall, eating candy
   • Grocery shopping, watching television, coughing.

7. Observe people participating in a variety of life situations. These observations can take place through reading, videos, television programs, and through firsthand contact. Make a list of these life situations and the actions that people take. State whether these action are likely to increase their risk to harm or decrease it (self, others, and the environment):
   • Smoking tobacco products
   • Running red lights
   • Consuming alcohol
   • Playing golf in a lightning storm

- Burning leaves on a dry day
- Pushing someone during a disagreement
- Expressing anger
- Cutting in line at the movies.

8. Teach your children five risk-management strategies they can use to lower their exposure to danger with respect to themselves, others, and the environment (seven centers of care). These strategies are risk avoidance, risk prevention, risk reduction, risk protection, and risk acceptance.

Risk Avoidance: When a life situation or activity is deemed dangerous and the risk of harm (self, others, or the environment) is high, a wise choice is to avoid involvement. Example: Tom avoids riding his bicycle when he does not have a protective helmet. Discussion: Ask your children to describe situations, events, or activities they would avoid because the risk for harm is too high.

Risk Prevention: These are choices (strategies) that children can use to lower their risk to danger before they participate in the life situation, activity, or event. Example: Susan wants to pass her next math test, so she thinks of all the things she can do in the days before the exam to help ensure a good grade. What are some risk-prevention choices that Susan can make to increase her chances of receiving a passing grade? Discussion: Ask your children to name some risk-prevention choices they can make to lower their risk of "catching" a cold.

Risk Reduction: These are choices that children can make to lower their risk of harm while participating in the life situation, activity, or event. Example: Brent makes the following choices while hiking in the woods with his parents: he walks at the same pace so as not to fall behind; he watches for trail markers so he won't get lost; and he looks where he steps so he will not fall down. Discussion: Ask your children what choices they can make while riding their bicycle to lower their risk of harm (control speed, watch for potholes, and maintain a safe distance from other riders).

Risk Protection: These are choices that children can make to care for themselves physically and emotionally. Example: Jill wears gloves, a protective helmet, and pads when she rollerblades. Steven has learned some self-care protection strategies like eating healthy foods, exercising, and getting a flu shot annually. Kelly has learned to protect her rather fragile ego by using rational thinking skills, positive self-talk, and relaxation training. Discussion: Ask your children to name some choices they can make to protect themselves physically and emotionally (riding bicycles, illness protection, bully protection, self put-down protection and name calling protection).

Risk Acceptance: This is a choice that children make when they understand the dangers to which they are exposed, have thoroughly investigated all that they can do to lower those risks, and now judge the level of danger sufficiently low to accept the exposure to danger. Example: Jimmy wants to ride a bicycle. He investigates the dangers associated with this activity. He learns about all the choices he can make to lower his risk of being harmed. He now judges bicycle riding to be relatively safe and accepts the risks. Discussion: Ask your children to name the steps they can take before accepting risk (know the activity, identify the dangers, and outline the steps they can take to lower these dangers). Judge whether the risk is still too high or is acceptable.

Younger children (ages five through nine) might have difficulty comprehending these five risk-management strategies. For children in this age group, concentrate on helping them identify the dangers and ideas they have for lowering them.

9. Now that your children understand that they can increase their safety and lower their risk to danger using effective risk-management strategies, give them an opportunity to use the five risk-management strategies they have learned. First, have them identify the potential dangers and then use as many of the five risk-management strategies that apply to these situations:
   - Smoking tobacco products
   - Swimming
   - Staying home alone
   - Picking up trash along the road
   - Peer pressure
   - Making friends
   - Taking a walk in the woods
   - Saving money to buy something.

10. Teach your children how to use Stop, Think, & Go decision mak-
    ing to lower their risk to danger. Use "Susan's Dilemma" on pp.
    192–194 and handout 5.1 on pg. 174 to teach each step of this de-
    cision-making method to your children.

6

GIVING AND RECEIVING CARE

BACKGROUND INFORMATION

Teaching Kids to Care and to Be Careful has been about helping children find purpose and meaning in their lives as givers and receivers of care. It has been about helping them experience personally the joys of life and living that come through caring and giving. Also, it has been about helping children to become caring human beings and builders of caring communities.

Understanding the Need for Givers and Receivers of Care

Giving and receiving care is at the core of our nature. It is what makes us human. Children are motivated to achieve social interest in their desire to belong, to contribute, and to secure a meaningful place in the groups to which they belong (home, school, and community). The significance of this nature is validated in five developmental life tasks that all human beings seek to attain (Mosak 1995).

1. They want meaningful relationships with others (friendships).
2. They want to make a contribution (to give to others).

3. They want a life of intimacy (love and caring family relationships).
4. They want to get along with themselves (self-acceptance).
5. They want to foster a spiritual essence, a life of purpose, and a meaningful relationship with the universe.

These five life tasks relate to nurturing children's caring nature, in which they learn to give and receive care in the context of being careful. The significant adults in children's lives are thus challenged with teaching them how to develop a sense of social significance through caring.

In the absence of social interest, children are likely to be motivated by self-interest and to lack purpose and meaning. A personal identity crisis is likely to emerge in which children face a life of confusion with little or no direction. Consequently, children must understand the significance of caring and how it contributes to their development as caring human beings.

Fostering a Life of Care

In teaching children to give and receive care, the focus must be on children not academic subject matter. What children learn about caring needs to be taught and experienced in the context of life lessons, not classroom lessons. Children will be best served when they understand how what they are learning in class relates to the caring choices they make at home, in school, and in their communities (local, state, national, and global). Only when children acknowledge their caring attitudes, skills, and personalities and apply them in their daily lives can we say that we have nurtured caring children who:

- Respect the rights of others
- Get along with themselves
- Experience a sense of belonging and social usefulness
- Understand their personal strengths and limitations
- Know their specific interests and talents
- Demonstrate effective interpersonal skills
- Function effectively in their roles as student, family member, friend, worker, volunteer, and so forth

- Understand the relationship of classroom to life learning in shaping their life experiences as givers and receivers of care
- Contribute to the life of their homes, schools, and communities
- Understand that it takes the collective contribution of all people to sustain a fully functioning and caring society
- Live lives of purpose and meaning through caring (Worzbyt, O'Rourke, & Dandeneau 2003).

Fostering a life of caring is captured in the preceding five chapters. Children become caring people when they recognize that life has value (chapter 1), that caring occurs in seven centers of care (chapter 2), that helpful and hurtful habits shape the caring choices that they make (chapter 3), that there is danger in caring (chapter 4), and that they can live full and productive lives through caring in the context of being careful (chapter 5).

A Blueprint for Caring

Fostering a life of caring involves the home, school, and community in providing children with opportunities to discover their purpose and the value of life; explore the infinite numbers of caring choices available to them; and obtain the "know how" to plan and implement caring activities, large and small. When these three elements come together, children will be able to accept more active roles in giving and receiving care.

Discovering My Purpose

You are helping your children to discover their purpose through a life-long journey of self-discovery guided by four life-defining questions that are integral and dynamic features of this book. These questions and your children's answers to them will help them to create a caring identity:

- What do I want to *be?*
- What do I want to *do?*
- What do I want to *have?*
- What do I want to *give?*

Throughout the previous weeks, you have been helping your children to *be* caring people, doing what caring people *do,* so that they will *have* much to *give*—the very best of what they have received. As givers and receivers of care, children become full participants in the circle of care, which helps them define their caring nature and shape a caring world.

Help your children appreciate what they have received, the relationships they have developed, and the quality of life they have come to enjoy. Remind them that they are the sum total of all that they have experienced. Their personality attributes, attitudes, values, and strengths, which others have helped shape, are now theirs to share with the world. Help your children stay focused on the four life-defining questions and use them as guides in continuing to reinvent themselves as caring human beings and builders of caring communities.

Exploring My Caring Possibilities

Giving and receiving care is first about helping children understand that they have been given much and therefore have much to give. Most children, if given the opportunity, strive to be kind-hearted bearers of caring and positive forces for responsible change. However, caring hearts and hands are not likely to achieve their true potential when children's actions are thwarted by failure to pursue the many caring possibilities that are open to them.

The opportunities to do good are vast and wide, the possibilities to make a difference are real and significant, and the caring outcomes are life defining and character building. If children are to develop a lifestyle of caring and commit themselves to lives of learning, service, and social justice, they must be exposed to caring opportunities in the seven centers of care and supported in their desire to have positive and caring impacts in their homes, schools, and communities.

We must work with our children in helping them to increase their awareness of the many ways in which they can offer what they *have* to *give* in support of caring and community building. We can involve them in caring practices that need to be continued. We can challenge them to look for hurtful and dangerous practices that need to be stopped, and involve them in stopping them. Also, we can encourage them to practice new caring choices that need to be implemented.

Planning to Care

The third and final step in the blueprint for caring is planning to care. We want our children to succeed in their caring endeavors, enjoy the journey, take pride in their accomplishments, and achieve their caring outcomes in the context of being careful. What follows are some tips and suggestions to consider as you help your children plan to care.

1. Help your children to name their strengths, attributes, interests, and things they enjoy doing. Review with them all that they have learned at home, in school, and in their communities in helping them to prepare their lists.
2. Guide your children in brainstorming a number of caring activities they can accomplish at home, in school, and in their communities (local, national, global). Use the seven centers of care in helping them to generate ideas.
3. Assist your children in matching their caring attributes with the caring opportunities (home, school, and community) that they have identified.
4. Ask your children to review their caring attributes and opportunities to care. Have them select caring choices in which they would like to become involved.
5. Some of your children's caring activities will require little planning. They represent the little things in life that pay big dividends in helping others care and become builders of caring communities. Examples of these activities include:
   - Smiling at others
   - Saying "thank you," "may I," and "please"
   - Taking turns
   - Listening to others
   - Giving compliments
   - Offering family and friends a helping hand.
6. When caring activities require planning, help your children think through the following questions: *Who* will benefit from this caring activity? *Why* is this an important act of care? *What* steps will I need to take to complete this activity? *When* will I begin and complete this act of care? *Where* will this act of care take place? and *How* will I know when I have succeeded?

7. Depending on the complex nature of a particular act of care, here
   are seven additional questions to consider:
   - Will I need the help of others and is help available?
   - How much time will be needed, and do I have the time to give?
   - Will this activity require funding, how much, and is it available?
   - Will I need to obtain clearances and permissions before I can
     begin?
   - Are there any specific dangers associated with this act of care,
     and can the risks be successfully managed?
   - Is this something I really want to do?
   - Who can help me take the first step?

Giving and receiving care is as important to life and living as the air we
breathe. Without caring, life would not hold promise, excitement, or
purpose. Caring is why we get out of bed each morning and anticipate
the excitement of each new day. Help your children plan a life of caring,
and they will gain as much as they give.

ROLE OF FACILITATOR

Ideally, *Teaching Kids to Care and to Be Careful* has given you cause to
reflect on the importance of caring and the central role that it plays in
children's lives. Caring is what children do. It is their purpose for
being, and it is what gives their lives meaning. All that we do as human
beings is care and be cared for by others. This rich cycle of giving and
receiving care contributes to the growth and well-being of all people
who participate in the process.

Help your children understand how important it is for them to become givers and receivers of care. Help them value and acknowledge
the care that they have been given and demonstrate their appreciation for what they have received. Help them understand that caring is
a reciprocal process in which givers and receivers of care respect and
acknowledge this special union. Caring works best when children
value and appreciate the gift of life and the opportunity to share with
others the gifts they have received. Therefore, encourage your children to partake fully in all that life has to give and to return in full
measure all that they have been given. Above all, be open to what

your children have to share. You can learn much from them, as they have much to give—and they will learn that their caring contributions are valued by others.

Chapter 6, "Giving and Receiving Care," is the last chapter of this book. However, it is a chapter without an ending. You and your children will continue to script your own lifelong adventure and a lifetime of discovering new opportunities for giving and receiving care. The suggestions, ideas, and activities that follow will help you help your children care more deeply and live life more fully as they make caring choices in support of their home, school, and community. Enjoy participating in these caring experiences and have fun making the last chapter of this book the most important chapter in children's lives.

ACTIVITIES

Caring Opportunities: Exploring the Possibilities

Objectives

1. To help children understand the many caring choices they can make at home, in school, and in their communities
2. To encourage children to make more caring choices and to participate in caring activities in support of their homes, schools, and communities.

Group size: Many of the caring opportunities available to children can be done alone, with families, in classroom-sized groups, and with community groups and organizations.

Time required: Some caring choices can be performed in seconds, while others will be open ended and ongoing.

Facilitator: The opportunities to give and receive care are endless. Now that your children understand that they are givers and receivers of care, they are ready to use all that they have been given in support of the seven centers of care. They understand that they must be receptive to receive what others have to give before they can pass on to others what they have been given.

Help your children understand how the cycle of giving and receiving care contributes to their own development as caring human beings and how their actions help others develop their caring natures as well.

Explain to your children that they have a responsibility to learn as much as they can and to give all that they can. Help them understand that they are contributing members of the circle of care, which depends on the willingness of all its members to give and receive care, share fully and unconditionally, and hold nothing back in support of a caring global environment.

Help your children understand that they are key players in maintaining the balance of nature. The choices they make will either enhance the quality of life or weaken the circle of care that supports their essences as caring human beings and builders of caring communities.

Process

1. Help your children to create a three-ring binder "Caring Choices" handbook. Divide this handbook into three sections: home, school, and community.
2. Use the question, "How do I want my home, school, and community to *be*?" Help your children describe what *caring* looks like in each of these environments.
3. Ask your children to describe what caring people must *do* to have a caring home, school, and community.
4. Explain to your children that they are now ready to begin brainstorming caring ideas, activities, and opportunities that they can use and share with others in support of creating caring homes, schools, and communities. Help your children focus on the seven centers of care as these centers influence caring in all three environments (home, school, and community).
5. Parents, teachers, and community members are valuable resources in developing the "Caring Choices" handbook. Involve the caring support of others in adding caring ideas to each section of the handbook. Involve your children in selecting caring choices they can make by themselves, with their parents (caregivers), with their peers, and with community groups and organizations.
6. The three following sections contain ideas, activities, and opportunities to consider when helping children to develop their "Caring

Choices" handbook. Consider these suggestions and add your own ideas in helping to create caring homes, schools, and communities.

20 Ways to Make Home a Caring Place to Be

Explore with your children the importance of being a caring person. Help them understand that everything they do begins with a choice. Encourage them to think before they act so they can make caring choices.

Home is where children first experience the care of others and where they learn to care. Home is where children develop loving and caring family relationships, foster meaningful and lasting connections with others, make valued and caring contributions in support of their families, develop self-acceptance, and first discover their purpose for being—to give and receive care.

The following caring experiences are important for children to have if they are to become caring people. They are listed in no particular order, but do reflect caring in the seven centers of care. Teach your children to:

- Care for themselves
- Care for family and friends
- Care for acquaintances and distant others
- Care for nonhuman animals
- Care for plants and the environment
- Care for the human-made world of objects and instruments
- Care for ideas.

1. Give smiles and words of encouragement.
2. Make a list of things you can do to care for yourself. Check the ones that you currently do and circle new caring choices that you will start today. Share your self-care list with others (family, friends, family doctor, etc.) and ask them to help you add more ideas to your list.
3. Discuss the meaning of "gift." Name some gifts you have given and received. Now think of some gifts that you can give daily that cost nothing but are treasured by those who receive them. Here are a few ideas:
   - Hugs

- Time
- Pats on the back
- Smiles
- Helping hands
- Thank you
- Kind words
- Compliments
- Saying "I love you."

These are gifts that you can "keep on giving." Get into the habit of giving these gifts daily and experience the joy of giving and receiving.

4. Look at your hands. See how they move and what they do. Hands are special when they are used for caring. Make a list of all the things that "caring hands" can do in helping to make home a caring place to be. Think about the seven centers of care as you make your "caring hands" list. Use your hands to care in the context of being careful.

5. Caring in five minutes a day is something that everyone can do, and it adds up to a lot of caring time in a year. Think of caring things that you can do in five minutes or less each day that will show your family that you care. Here are a few ideas:
   - Wash your own dishes and return them to the cupboard
   - Make your bed
   - Place dirty clothes in the hamper
   - Feed and water your pet
   - Write mom and dad a thank-you note for being good parents.

6. Home rules are caring rules that may be misunderstood. List your home rules and how they help the family to give and receive care:
   - Call home if you're going to be late
   - Turn off lights that are not being used
   - Put things back where you find them
   - Keep your room clean
   - Do your chores
   - Eat meals together.

7. Keep a stack of "thank you" cards available at all times. Make a habit of giving thanks to those who care.

8. Hold family meetings once a week to discuss the caring choices that family members have been making. Celebrate each other's acts of care and how giving and receiving care is helping your family become the caring family it wants to be. Plan new acts of care to be implemented during the coming week.

9. Practice "what if" scenarios together at home. This activity will help you to problem solve real life situations before they become a reality. Here are a few "what if" situations to consider. Keeping caring and safety in mind, identify the potential dangers for each situation and the caring choices that you can make to lower the risk of harm to yourself, others, and the environment:
   • What if someone knocks at the front door and you are home alone?
   • What if you want to talk with someone about your feelings?
   • What if your brother or sister hurts you?
   • What if you find paper lying on the ground?
   • What if you read about someone in your community who has lost everything because their house has burned?

10. Look for things that your family can do to make your home a caring and safe place to be. Contact your local fire department and ask for a home safety inspection checklist. Look for home dangers and things your family can do to reduce the danger and increase family safety.

11. Your home is filled with objects and instruments that are designed to care. What must you do to care for them so that they will care for you?

12. Create a conversation jar. Brainstorm a list of caring topics that are important and will be fun for your family to discuss. Write each topic on a three-by-five index card and place these cards in a large open mouth jar. At dinner time, or in the evening, make a habit of pulling one card from the jar and have a family discussion. Possible topics might include:
   • The importance of being a volunteer
   • Love
   • Sharing
   • Helping others
   • Places I would like to go.

13. Families that care for each other share in the household chores. Make a list of the household chores that need to be done. Discuss how completing these chores help the family care for itself. Select a family chore from the list and perform it for one week. Each week select a new chore to perform. Discuss what it is like to perform these chores and what it is like to benefit from the chores that other family members perform. Use family meeting times for these discussions.

14. Create a caring home environment in which everyone feels comfortable. Work together to hang family photographs and pictures. Decorate living spaces using color, fabrics, favorite objects, and so on.

15. Practice your caring behaviors beyond your home. Model acts of caring at the mall, at your doctor's office, at school, and in your community. Care for people that you don't know by using good manners, helping hands, and treating them with respect through sharing, taking turns, listening, offering compliments, and giving "warm fuzzies" (smiles, kind words, handshakes, etc.).

16. Become involved in community service. While your family needs to care for itself, its members can build strong family ties by volunteering together in support of each other. Families can help neighbors do chores around the home. They can visit nursing homes and help care for those who can no longer care for themselves. They can join community service groups, like the YMCA, that support a variety of community service projects. Select a project that interests you and your family, and volunteer together, in an act of caring for your school or community.

17. Pets are family members too. Discuss how your pets care for you. They give you pleasure and unconditional love, and they help you to reduce you stress. While your pets give you much, what must you give them in return? Do all that you can do in caring for your pets.

18. Families develop close ties when they vacation together and enjoy the environment through such activities as hiking, skiing (snow and water), boating, fishing, and sightseeing. Discuss how your environment cares for you and gives you pleasure. With all that your environment gives you, what must you give in return in order to maintain this caring relationship? Become involved in caring projects that support a healthy, caring environment.

19. Many families enjoy gardening together. Planting crops is fun, and the crops provide a healthy food source. Plants and flowers are enjoyable to observe. They prevent soil erosion and help provide the clean air that you breathe. Discuss all that plants give to a quality family life. Think about all the caring choices that you can make in support of the plant life in you area. Do all that you can to care for plants so they will continue to care for you.

20. Caring ideas give life direction. Caring ideas support families in their quest to care for each other. List some caring ideas that help families to become strong caring families. Discuss these ideas and care for them through your actions:
    - Love your neighbor as yourself
    - Treat others as you would like to be treated
    - Take time to care
    - Take turns
    - Wear you seat belt
    - Exercise daily
    - Spend quality time together
    - A family that works and plays together stays together
    - Caring gives life purpose and direction.

25 Ways to Make School a Caring Place to Be

Children want to belong, to be a part of something larger than themselves, to feel safe and secure, and to experience a sense of predictability in their lives. They want to like themselves, to be liked by others, and to give of themselves in helping to create caring classrooms and caring school communities. Most of all, they want to live a life of meaning and purpose through giving and receiving care.

Children want to become members of caring school communities where they can relax, are unafraid to take risks, and where they feel comfortable in revealing themselves to others. They want to be able to ask for help when they need it and to share with others their hopes, dreams, inadequacies, hurts, and fears knowing that they will receive support. They want to be in classrooms where they can share their accomplishments knowing that their classmates will acknowledge with pride, delight, and admiration their successes.

Children want to be in classrooms where there is open communication, where they feel comfortable being themselves, and where they are free to discuss their concerns, problems, and desires free from retribution or exclusion. They want to be in classrooms where they can build strong caring peer ties; where they can have opportunities to work, play, and socialize together; and where they can cooperatively problem solve in fostering shared goals the likes of which will help them create a caring community where everyone feels connected, needed, and valued for being themselves.

Children want to be members of caring classrooms and school communities where inclusion, team building, and cooperation are practiced and where competition and exclusion are viewed as barriers to community building and are therefore discouraged. The activities, suggestions, and tips that follow are designed for teachers to help children become caring people and builders of caring school communities, people who give and receive care in the context of being careful.

1. Conduct brief, daily classroom meetings to discuss how children want their classroom to be and what they can do to make it happen. Children are encouraged to discuss their feelings, concerns, joys, achievements, and hopes for the day. They are likewise encouraged to offer support to others, words of encouragement, and compliments.

2. Teach children to give and receive compliments and provide time on a daily basis to do so.

3. Discuss the meaning of tolerance and understanding. Explore ways in which both can be implemented and then implement some of these ideas.

4. Plan an ethnic-awareness day, week, or month. Invite people of diversity to share their customs, food, clothing, literature, art, and dance.

5. Create "warm fuzzies" and caring recognition awards, and have children give them away to those who demonstrate acts of caring.

6. Develop a plan for welcoming new children to your classroom. Decide what caring actions can be taken to help new children feel connected to your school, teachers, and children.

7. Create "New Kid Survival Kits." Decide what should go into these kits, which will help newly admitted children to care for

themselves, meet teachers and administrators, make friends, and connect with their school in positive ways. Make these kits and distribute them to newcomers.

8. Establish a buddy system for new students and for children returning to school after being away for a while. Buddies can be there to talk, answer questions, help with schoolwork, and make friends or reestablish old connections.

9. Evaluate your school lunch program. Ask your school nurse to help you make a checklist that can be used in conducting your evaluation. Review the results, compliment your cafeteria staff for their care, and offer some suggestions for improving the school lunch program.

10. Plan and organize an after-school exercise club. Work with your health and physical education teacher in creating your plan.

11. Contact various health organizations in your community. Find out what services they can offer children. Invite one or more of these organizations to meet with your class or school in planning a schoolwide health fair in which children can participate.

12. Make "I Care Kits" for the homeless, hospitalized, people in nursing homes, and newcomers to your community. Discuss what these kits might contain, how these items can be obtained, and what steps should be taken in preparing and delivering them to those in need.

13. Help set up and manage a classroom or schoolwide tutoring program.

14. Plan, organize, and implement an after-school bicycle-safety clinic.

15. Plan, organize, and implement a "home alone" caring and safety program.

16. Make a flyer listing "after-school safety tips" for younger children. Distribute the flyers to parents and children.

17. Inspect your school playground for dangers and report them to your school principal.

18. Write reports and conduct mini-workshops for parents and children on such topics as:
    - Playing It Safe on the Playground
    - Swimming: Playing It Cool in the Pool

- Peddling Bicycle Safety
- Seat Belts: Buckle Up for Safety
- Walking My Way to Safety.

19. Help organize a Safe Babysitting Class. Your local YMCA and Red Cross chapters can help with this program.

20. Help to organize a "safe walking" program in which younger children are escorted to school by older children.

21. Organize a school beautification club. These children can plant flowers and trees, keep the schoolyard free of litter, and work with school custodians to perform other tasks as needed.

22. Create a list of classroom and schoolwide jobs that will help to promote caring and safety. Some examples are the following:
    - Classroom and school greeters. These children greet children with a smile and a warm hello when coming to school and leaving school at the end of the day.
    - "Missing persons patrol." These children keep track of children who are absent from school and see that they receive "missing you" cards, welcome them back to school, and help them to catch up on what they have missed.
    - Messengers. These children run errands for the teacher.
    - "Helpful hands." These children function as school tutors. They offer assistance with school work.
    - "Peer buddies." These children support new children. They stay with them for a year and help them to adjust to their new surroundings.

23. Create classroom student councils and one for the school. Student council children work to create caring and safe classrooms and caring and safe school climates. They take suggestions from their peers and observe the day-to-day life experiences of children looking for ways to support cooperation, inclusion, and caring in school.

24. Look for caring projects to plan and implement in the seven centers of care. Each center can be enhanced through the active participation of children who use what they have learned at home and in school to care and be careful.

25. Create a caring school environment. Think of ways in which music, art, color, literature, sayings, and pictures can help to contribute to

a warm and caring physical environment. Brainstorm many ideas, to include the following, which will help promote caring:

- Hang wall pictures and posters that demonstrate caring.
- Create caring spaces where children can go to calm down, connect with their peers, and relax.
- Create class songs, cheers, logos, and banners to celebrate caring and cooperation.
- Make a caring thermometer that measures the caring atmosphere in the classroom. Move the index often (hot, warm, lukewarm, cold) to measure the climate. Use this information to engage the class in problem-solving ways to improve climatic conditions.
- Create a caring-word wall. Every time children use a caring word or discover a new one, it goes on the wall as a reminder to use these words often. Caring sayings can also be placed on the caring-word wall.
- Create a "caring jar" with slips of paper stacked beside the jar. When children do something of a caring nature or "catch others" doing the same, they identify the caring act, who did it, and place the slips in the jar. At the end of each day, children read allowed the name of children who cared and what they did. Establish a "Caring Wall Hall of Fame." Include the names of children, teachers, and community members who care.

Classrooms and schools can become caring places to be when the people in them give and receive care in the context of being careful. Help your children use what they have learned about caring to care for themselves, others, and their school environment.

20 Ways to Make My Community a Caring Place to Be

Life is sustained through a delicately balanced ecosystem that is maintained by a circle of care. To the extent that children make caring choices in the seven centers of care, they help to sustain that delicate balance. When this balance is threatened through a lack of responsible caring, the results are poverty, war, unemployment, illness, disease, political unrest, oppression, and inequities of all kinds, producing human suffering that first threatens the safety and security of individuals and eventually communities, local and global.

Children are integral and valued participants in the circle of care. They affect and are affected by the life choices that they and others make. We teach children the value of caring for themselves but rarely involve them as full and significant players in helping to shape caring communities. Because children are motivated by social interest at a very early age, it behooves communities (local and global) to take more active roles in helping children to develop a sense of belonging, cooperation, and inclusion by experiencing and participating in activities that will help enrich and enhance community wellness.

Community leaders, teachers, and parents have an opportunity to work together in teaching children about their community—its strengths, weaknesses, opportunities, and the threats it faces. They can work together in identifying ways in which children can become actively involved in the life of their community and its care.

Children need to understand from an early age that they have much to give and receive from a community that cares for them and values their involvement. Communities must therefore find ways to involve their children in meaningful and responsible opportunities to care, sharing with others what they have to give. What follows are 20 things that children can do with adult guidance to support caring communities (local and global).

1. Participate in an "I Care Day." Brainstorm a list of caring things that you can do in a day for your community. Select caring activities like raking leaves, trimming bushes, sweeping sidewalks, and planting flowers. Then have fun caring for a day.
2. Attend a community council meeting. Learn about your community's needs and ways you can volunteer your time in caring for your community and the people who live in it.
3. Identify areas in your community that pose a danger to others (potholes, fallen limbs, playground equipment in disrepair, hidden traffic control signs, etc.). Contact people in your community who can address these dangers.
4. Form a "Kid Volunteers" group in your community. Assist people who need your help (elderly, people who are ill, and those who are

physically challenged). You can run errands, do household chores, do yard work, wash cars, etc.

5. Beautify your community. You can work with people in your community who are interested in giving your community a new look. Activities might include planting flowers, plants, and trees; painting fences; removing graffiti from buildings; and so on.

6. Work with your community parks and recreation agency. Improve stream beds, stock ponds and streams with fish, remove fallen trees, build safe hiking trails, and so on.

7. Organize a "Caring Kids—Caring Families" club to generate and implement ideas and projects to strengthen family and community life. Some possible projects are:
   • Sponsor weekly family recreation activities
   • Plan popcorn and movie nights
   • Promote a family health and wellness fair.

8. With the help of adults, conduct a community caring and safety survey for the purpose of generating ideas that will improve community caring and safety. The survey can be conducted at shopping malls, in downtown areas, community gatherings, and other places where people congregate. Survey results can be reviewed and implemented by individuals, families, and community groups.

9. Start a volunteer community crime watch program or participate in one that is already established in your community. Contact your local police department for assistance, training, and tips in reducing crime in your area.

10. Honor those who care with a card, letter, or some form of recognition. Start a "Caring Matters" column in your local newspaper as a way of recognizing people who care.

11. Publicize community holiday caring and seasonal safety tips. Help your community care and be careful when preparing food, using fireplaces, consuming alcohol, sledding, hunting, buying gifts, and so on. Use your newspaper, a community website, public television, radio spots, and local organizations to promote caring and safety tips.

12. Bring flowers, magazines, crossword puzzles, and entertainment to nursing and personal-care homes.

13. Read newspapers, stories, and magazine articles to those who can no longer read.

14. Send cards, letters, and care packages to people serving in our armed services. Contact your state legislators and post office for guidelines and suggestions in organizing these mailings.

15. Generate a list of caring ideas on which our country was founded. Read the Bill of Rights, the Preamble to the Constitution, Martin Luther King's "I Have a Dream" speech, and the Gettysburg Address for caring ideas. Discuss each idea listed and ways these caring ideas are kept alive today. Do what you can to care for these caring ideas.

16. Make "I Care Kits" for the homeless, senior citizens, the hospitalized, community newcomers, and so on. Brainstorm a list of items to include in each kit and distribute them to those in need.

17. Learn about the dangers that threaten local and global communities. Poverty, unemployment, hunger, illness and disease, war, terrorism, crime, environmental threats, natural disasters, and human rights violations are just some of the issues that local and world communities must address. Identify one or more of these areas in which you have an interest. Learn what you can do to care and who can help you to get started.

18. Become involved in local and national politics. Learn about the issues and the candidates. While you cannot cast a vote, you can volunteer your time to support candidates whose caring ideas you value and would like to see implemented.

19. Raise money to purchase and distribute "object and instrument kits" that promote caring and safety. Smoke and fire alarms, fire extinguishers, carbon monoxide detectors, batteries, flashlights, blankets, first aid kits, candles, matches, can goods, propane stoves, and emergency phone number cards are just a few of the many objects and instruments that families should have in their homes.

20. Help promote caring and inclusion in your community. Form discussion groups and activities that bring people of diversity together in the spirit of cooperation, understanding, and caring. Work with people in your community to promote ways to care for acquaintances and distant others.

Many acts of care are waiting to be developed, and new caregivers are waiting to be discovered. "When children recognize that the circle of caring begins with them and that the caring choices they make define themselves and the world, they will one day experience a kinder and more compassionate society with fewer personal, social, political, economic, and environmental ills, because they cared" (Worzbyt, O'Rourke, Dandeneau 2003, 469).

Classroom Caring Service Project

Objectives

1. To help children create, implement, and evaluate a classroom caring service project or individual service projects (one per child)
2. To help children experience the joy of being volunteers.

Group Size: Classroom group
Time: 30–45 minutes to discuss classroom caring project ideas. More time will be needed to implement the projects.
Materials: Create your own list of project ideas for kids
Facilitator: The purpose of this activity is to acquaint children with the vast number of opportunities that await them in which they can play a significant role in the care of others. Tell your children that they will be working together in selecting a caring project and then volunteering their services in seeing their caring service project through to completion.
Remind your children that it is not the size of their project that matters but rather their sincerity and unselfish willingness to give what they have to benefit others. The first step in this process will be to help your children understand the nature of volunteerism and the good feelings that people enjoy when they care for others. What follows are a variety of things that you can do to help your children identify service projects of interest.

Process

1. Ask your children to share with you their understanding of what it means to be a volunteer.

2. As you discuss volunteerism and the work that volunteers do, ask if any of them have volunteered their services to help others. Help them understand that acts of caring need not be major projects but can be random ways in which people do little things to care and to help others in being careful. Have your children brainstorm acts of caring that are being carried out by some adults and children every day. Some examples are:
   - Carrying groceries to cars
   - Raking leaves for someone
   - Sending cards ("get well," "thinking of you," "happy birthday")
   - Placing batteries in smoke and fire detectors
   - Reminding someone to wear their seat belt
   - Reporting information on missing road signs
   - Teaching someone how to make 911 emergency calls
   - Helping a friend to understand a class assignment
   - Picking up trash off the street.

3. Have your children discuss the many reasons why they think children and adults volunteer their time caring and helping others to be careful. "What's in it for them?"

4. Ask your children what they think would happen if everyone in their classroom individually volunteered his or her time to do one caring thing to help their classroom community.

5. Ask your children to identify one caring act (volunteering) they can carry out during the week that will benefit others or their environment in some small, but significant way. This can be a homework assignment in which children write their goals on index cards and carry them out during the week. At the close of each day, children can share their acts of caring.

6. Now that you have explored the importance of volunteerism and caring, tell your children that they will have an opportunity to make a positive difference in the lives of others by adopting a caring service activity which they can sponsor as a class project. You may have your children choose individual service projects to sponsor rather than manage one large project.

7. Identify a limited number of service project possibilities and share them with your children. Keep the projects simple in nature and suggest ones that can easily involve the participation of your class.

You may consider ideas shared in this chapter as well as ideas that you have received from your community.

8. Have your children discuss the ideas presented and select one project to implement.
9. Using the guidelines provided in this chapter, help your children create a service project action plan.
10. Implement and evaluate your plan.

Lesson Variation

Rather than develop a class caring project, you may choose to have your children discuss caring projects that they could do with family members, local social service agencies, or in their communities. With help from home, children can participate in a caring experience of their choosing and then share with classmates what they did and how they felt.

Discussion

1. Your children should be able to: define "volunteerism," understand the importance of being a volunteer in support of others and their environment, recognize that what they care for will one day care for them, and understand the implications for themselves and society when people cease to care and to be careful.
2. You can test their understanding of this material by asking: "What is a volunteer?" "What do volunteers do?" "Why is it important for all people to volunteer their time, money, and talents in support of caring?" "What would happen if each person in your home, school, community, county, and globally only cared for themselves and no one else?" "What can you do to help ensure that acts of caring not only continue but increase in number?"

REFERENCES

Erikson, E. H. (1963). *Children and society* (2nd ed.). New York: Norton.

Havinghurst, R. J. (1972). *Developmental tasks and education* (3rd ed.). New York: McKay.

Lipsitz, J. (1995). Why we should care about caring? (prologue). *Kappan,* 7, 665–66.

Maslow, H. A. (1954). *Motivation and personality.* New York: Harper and Row.

Mosak, H. H. (1995). Adlerian psychology. In R. J. Corisini & D. Wedding (eds.), *Current psychotherapies* (5th ed., pp. 51–94). Itasca, IL: F. E. Peacock.

Noddings, N. (1992). *The challenge to care in schools: An alternative approach to education.* New York: Teachers College Press.

———. (1995a). A morally defensible mission for schools in the 21st century. *Kappan,* 76, 365–368.

———. (1995b). Teaching themes of caring. *Kappan,* 7, 675–679.

O'Rourke, K., & J. C. Worzbyt (1996). *Support groups for children.* Washington, DC: Accelerated Development—A member of Taylor and Francis.

Pittman, K. J., & M. Cahill (1992). Youth and caring: The role of youth programs in the development of caring. Commissioned Paper for Lilly Endowment Youth and Caring Conference (February 26–27, 1992). Miami, FL: Center for Youth Development & Policy Research.

Sapon-Shevin, M. (1999). *Because we can change the world: A practical guide to building cooperative inclusive classroom communities.* Boston: Allyn & Bacon.

Thygerson, A. L. (1992). *Safety* (2nd ed.). Boston: Jones & Bartlett.

Worzbyt, J. C. (1991). *Beating the odds.* Altoona, PA: R.J.S. Films.

———. (1998). *Caring children make caring choices.* Harrisburg: Pennsylvania Department of Education.

Worzbyt, J. C., K. O'Rourke, & C. Dandeneau (2003). *Elementary school counseling: A commitment to caring and community building* (2nd ed.). New York: Brunner-Routledge.

INDEX

ABOUT THE AUTHOR

Dr. John C. Worzbyt is professor emeritus in the Counseling Department at Indiana University of Pennsylvania. During his 31 years of department service, he has been a former chairperson, coordinator of doctoral studies, and coordinator of school counseling certification programs. John has been an educator for 39 years, having worked as an elementary school teacher and middle school science teacher, elementary school counselor, and counselor educator. He received his advanced education degrees from the University of Rochester.

John has coauthored four previous counseling textbooks, three monographs, and school counseling articles on a variety of topics. He is in the process of completing a caring children activities book to be used by adult caregivers, working in a variety of settings, who strive to foster caring children and builders of caring communities.

Three of John's publications have received national writing awards from the American School Counselor Association and the former American Personnel and Guidance Association. His third coauthored publication, *Beating the Odds,* was honored and recognized by the United States Congressional Medal of Honor Society as its 1995 Youth Program of the Year.

John is a registrant of the National Distinguished Registry for Counseling and Development and has been listed in *Who's Who in the World,*

American Education, Directory of American Scholars, and *Who's Who in Medicine and Healthcare.* He is also a former recipient of the Counselor Educator of the Year Award (Pennsylvania School Counselor Association), the Eminent Practitioner Award (Pennsylvania Counseling Association), and the College of Education Faculty Recognition Award for Outstanding Accomplishments as Teacher-Scholar (Indiana University of Pennsylvania).

For the past several years, John has been a consultant, keynote speaker, and workshop presenter at state, regional, national, and international conferences. He has worked with school districts, hospitals, businesses, social service agencies, and mental health associations presenting programs in caring and community building, leadership training, and human potential enhancement.

John has been married to his wife, Jean, for 37 years. They have two grown children, Jason and Janeen, who work in higher education.